Looking at Barnett Newman

Looking at Barnett Newman
Jeremy Lewison

Published by August, London

First published in 2002
by August Media Ltd
116–120 Golden Lane
London EC1Y OTL, UK

A CIP catalogue record for
this book is available from
the Library of Congress,
Washington, D.C., USA.

Publishing director:
Nick Barley
Creative director:
Stephen Coates
Project editor: Alex Stetter
Editorial assistant:
Catherine Ford
Picture researcher: Juliet Duff

Repro by Precise@Icon
Printed by BAS Printers

Printed on acid-free paper
produced of chlorine-free
pulp. TCF ∞

ISBN 1-902854-20-9

9 8 7 6 5 4 3 2 1

www.augustmedia.co.uk

**Publisher's
acknowledgements**
Lexi Cherniavsky, Celia Clear,
Lise Connellan

**Author's
acknowledgements**
This essay was written in July
2001 and slightly revised in
April 2002. I would like to
thank Sophie Howarth who
acted as my assistant in the
early stages of research and
Stephen Grosz who read an
early draft of the text and
made some valuable
suggestions. A later draft was
read by David Mellor and I am
grateful to him for
encouraging me to publish it
and to Nick Barley for having
the vision to do so.
 The Barnett Newman
Foundation hold the
copyright for Newman's
works and writings and I
would like to thank John
O'Neill for permission to
reproduce them here. His
colleagues Heidi Colsman-
Freyberger and Sarah Henry
provided me with an
enormous amount of help on
the occasions I visited the
Foundation to research in the
archive and I am very grateful
to them. I am equally grateful
to Peter Stevens and Rebecca
Smith who, as on many
previous occasions,
generously hosted my stay in
New York during research
visits.
 Finally I would like to
thank my wife Caroline
Schuck for her support
throughout the project.
Without her there would be
no publication.
Jeremy Lewison

In memory of my mother,
Dinora Pines Lewison

Frontispiece:
Voice of Fire
1967
Acrylic on canvas
543.6 x 243.8 cm
National Gallery of Canada,
Ottawa

Cover:
Adam (detail)
1951–52
Oil on canvas
242.9 x 202.9 cm
Tate, London

Back cover:
Barnett Newman and an
unidentified woman with
Cathedra (1951)
in Newman's Front Street
studio, 1958. Photograph
by Peter A. Juley

Contents

Barnett Newman
looking at *Be I* (1949) at
his exhibition at Betty
Parsons Gallery, New
York, 1950. Photograph
by Aaron Siskind

Looking at Barnett Newman

I begin with a confession: I have always found the painting of Barnett Newman difficult. Difficult to understand, difficult to empathise with, difficult to penetrate. I am not the first person to feel this. Newman's first two exhibitions at Betty Parsons' gallery in New York were greeted with coolness by his contemporaries, perhaps with incomprehension or incredulity. They did not quite know what to make of it, where he fitted in. Recently Yve-Alain Bois also admitted that Newman was one of the most difficult artists he had written about.[1] Critics and writers have claimed Newman variously as an exemplar of high modernism, a late romantic, a practitioner of the art of the sublime, a precursor of Minimalism, an existentialist and a spiritual artist obsessed with Judaism and the Kabbalah. What this variety of approaches shows is that there is no definitive way of reading Newman and that in spite of the directives given by his writings he is open to a number of different approaches. Given an œuvre with an appearance of such consistency it is odd that it is difficult to grasp its entirety. Among the difficulties I have is deciding which approach is the correct one or, rather, whether there is a single approach to satisfy my quest for meaning.

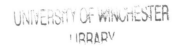

In general I might describe a typically mature Newman, one painted from 1949 onwards, as a field of colour (whether pigmented or not) interrupted by one or more vertical 'zips' or wider bands of (sometimes sharply, sometimes harmoniously) contrasting colour. From afar the painted field often appears even, although up close you can see that it is frequently inflected with brushstrokes. However, from a reasonable viewing distance the field looks blank. The 'zips', on the other hand, can have either ragged or clean edges. Of course, there are a number of paintings that do not fit this description where the field is disturbed by pronounced brushwork – for example, *Day before One* (1951), *Cathedra* (1951) and *Ulysses* (1952) – or where the field tails off and is 'incomplete' – for example, *Tertia* (1964) or *The Third* (1962). On the whole, however, the surfaces of Newman's paintings after 1950 are restrained. The overall effect is one of muteness: something forbidding, hermetic, unyielding, possibly boring. I have frequently stood before a Newman painting and asked myself what I derive from it and have found myself feeling numb and disturbed by my lack of response. Yet I also find that I am compelled to stay there, to dwell on my response, staring into blankness and feeling myself unnerved by the contemplation of nothing. For Jean-François Lyotard, the French philosopher, the message of Newman's paintings '"speaks" of nothing; it emanates from no one. ... The message is the presentation, but it presents nothing.'[2] There is in effect nothing other than what you see. 'Everything is there – dimensions, colours, lines – but there are no allusions. So much so that it is a problem for the commentator. What can one say that is not given? It is not difficult to describe, but the description is a flat paraphrase.'[3]

Perhaps the most celebrated example of the 'flat paraphrase' is Donald Judd's article on Newman written in 1964 in which, more or less, he does nothing but describe the look of the paintings.[4] Since the role of the commentator is to comment, not to describe, Newman's painting apparently renders Judd redundant. While Judd might have been comfortable with this, other contemporary commentators have expressed their discomfort on looking at Newman's paintings. The artist Allen Kaprow suggested that Newman's painting 'makes us psychically and physically exposed'.[5] Exposure is uncomfortable. The art historian Barbara Reise announced her discomfort in a letter to Newman: 'I *still* cannot face your paintings for any length of time'(her italics).[6]

The feeling of discomfort arises in part from rebuff and in part from concealment. Something seems to be hidden from the viewer. In 1972, Harold Rosenberg, later the author of a monograph on Newman, characterised Newman's painting as 'partly inaccessible'.[7] There is no way in; a painting by Newman is a barrier. The critic Peter Plagens described Newman's painting as 'a coloured wall', while his colleague, Barbara Rose, earlier referred to it as an 'impenetrable façade'.[8] Unlike the paintings of his contemporary, Mark Rothko, a mature work by Newman rarely permits the viewer to enter a space beyond the picture in time and place. Newman holds the viewer in the here and now, in front of a barrier he cannot transcend.

The titles of a number of Newman's works are a clear indication of his intentions in this regard: *Here, Be, Now, Moment, Right Here* to name only some of them. Newman acknowledged that modern painting in the first half of the twentieth century had destroyed the third dimension, 'preventing us from entering the picture and thus keeping us outside, compelling us to contemplate the painter's language and thereby forcing us to react to the painter's use of language.'[9] The result, according to Newman, was the disappearance of any subject other than language itself. This was a condition of sickness he set out to remedy.

Trained as a philosopher, Newman's writings are conceptual in as much as they declare a programme for art before he actually enacted it. He described the new American painting as 'philosophic',[10] an art of ideas. Newman talked about returning to the beginning and identified with the artists of so-called 'primitive' cultures. Yet his painting has been regarded as exemplary of the tradition of modernist reduction towards what became known as literalism – painting that was self-referential, dealing with aspects unique to the properties of painting: flatness and colour. His art was thus conceptually sophisticated. For Newman, however, the issue was not how to paint but what to paint. At the height of the Second World War he declared: 'If we could describe the art of this, the first half of the twentieth century, in a phrase, it would read as "the search for something to paint".'[11] Only the Surrealists, according to Newman, were successful in maintaining an interest in the subject but they had reached a 'cul-de-sac of invention'.[12] Their fantasies were incapable of describing the actuality of the horrors of the post-war, post-Holocaust world he inhabited. Newman was clear about what he wanted to paint. His quest was for an adequate means to express it.

For some commentators there is no doubt about the meaning of Newman's paintings. For example, Thomas Hess sought a way in through Newman's titles and, indeed, Newman himself suggested that his titles were a clue to the meaning of his work, although it is now known that Newman did not attribute titles to many of his works until 1958.[13] Hess conceived that Newman's paintings are underpinned by the latter's interest in the Kabbalah and numerology, and express a profound belief in Judaism and numinosity. In spite of Newman's widow's refutation of his interpretation and of Hess's inaccuracy in measuring intervals between 'zips' that led him to propose a secret mathematics as the fundamental structural basis of Newman's art, it is hard to discount it entirely. Even if at times his interpretation is a little fanciful, it is not totally implausible, not least because Hess delivered his theory with such commitment. Newman himself urged the art critic 'not ... to create a work of science or even a work of art, but that each time he writes, [to] create himself'. The critic, Newman asserted, should follow Baudelaire's dictum to be 'partial, passionate, political' (Newman's italics).[14] He should be free to say what he likes. Hess's work is nothing if not passionate and perhaps reveals as much about his own interests as Newman's. But what more can one ask of a commentator? There is never a definitive answer to the question 'what does this painting mean?' The best that can be offered is 'this is what it means to me given how it is painted, the context in which it was made, the circumstances in which I am viewing it and the state of mind that I am in now'.

* * *

I am standing in front of *Onement I*. I see a maroon field (Indian red) split by an orange vertical stripe (cadmium red light). The field has an uneven, relatively thin paint film; the orange stripe has a thick impasto and is painted onto and overlaps a piece of masking tape. It is a searing orange, a somewhat painful interjection into a field of doleful colour. It stands proud, a form against a ground, and in this it is almost, although not quite, unique in Newman's œuvre. I look at the painting and stare into its blankness. I could move on because I have seen all there is to see but I linger in the hope that it will reveal something more. As I continue to

Onement I
1948
Oil on canvas and oil on masking tape on canvas
69.2 x 41.2 cm
The Museum of Modern Art, New York. Gift of Annalee Newman, 1992

II

12

look I become aware of myself in the act of looking. The blankness and the singularity of the image refer me back to myself. The vertical band reminds me of my own verticality and I begin to connect myself to the painting. I start to feel self-conscious and to sense my own presence in the room. I look at the object in front of me and it provokes a feeling of discomfort, as though I am looking into a mirror.

Before *Onement I* Newman's paintings were concerned with Creation myths. Their antecedents were a mix of European Surrealism and the work of American painters such as Arthur Dove and Georgia O'Keefe.[15] These are pictures in the sense of depicting some kind of mythical scene in the making, the birth of the world, to use a title of a well-known painting by Miró, whom Newman admired. *Onement I* represented a sharp break from that and, whatever arguments are put forward about a possible debt to Giacometti,[16] Newman was taking a big leap. He was aware of that, for having painted the orange zip he stopped painting for nine months to consider what he had done. His previous practice, when painting *The Command* (1946), for example, had been to pull off the tape and then paint the zip directly onto the canvas but this time something prevented him from doing so. It was probably a sense of rightness about the mark, a recognition of something he could not yet understand and a fear that he would not be able to repeat the quality of the stroke or the relationship between the two paint films a second time. The cadmium red light had overlapped the tape and he had gone too far to be able to pull it off and replicate the effect. I think he was also disturbed by his creation.

It is not the satisfaction or indeed the inability to repeat the act that concerns me here. It is the act of looking, of contemplating the image for a long period before releasing the work into the world that are of interest. Newman explained to the art critic David Sylvester that he painted *Onement I* on his birthday in 1948. 'What happened there was that I'd done this painting and stopped in order to find out what I had done, and I actually lived with that painting for almost a year trying to understand it. I realised that I'd made a statement which was affecting me and which was, I suppose, the beginning of my present life, because from then on I had to give up any relation to nature, as seen.'[17]

Newman's account, seventeen years after the event, may be apocryphal and may represent an attempt to erect a myth around the simplest of gestures, but there is no evidence to disprove its veracity. Indeed he

Opposite:
Genesis – The Break
1946
Oil on canvas
61 x 68.9 cm
Dia Center for the Arts,
New York

repeated it in an interview shortly before he died.[18] A painting executed on his birthday marks the beginning of his life, a nice coincidence perhaps but also, in retrospect, a moment of significance. In the act of continuous looking Newman becomes aware of what he has done, becomes acquainted with the image and familiar with what he has projected onto the canvas. Newman continued: 'To verbalise and articulate what I think the line did to me, what *Onement* made me realise is that I was confronted for the first time with the thing that I did, whereas up until that moment I was able to remove myself from the act of painting, or from the painting itself.'[19] His reference to confrontation and to being able previously to remove himself from the painting suggests that here, in *Onement I,* Newman confronts himself. He looks at the painting and he sees himself reflected. It is a Hegelian moment of recognition when the self recognises that the other 'has come out of itself'.[20]

The time that elapsed between the execution of the work and the recognition that it was 'a thing' has interesting parallels with the theory of the 'mirror stage'. According to the French psychoanalyst Jacques Lacan, in a paper written in 1949,[21] the 'mirror stage', which occurs between six and eighteen months in the life of a child, is the period when the infant begins to recognise himself in the mirror. Unlike a chimpanzee, which soon tires of its discovery, the infant explores it 'in a series of gestures in which he experiences in play the relation between the movements assumed in the image and the reflected environment, and between this virtual complex and the reality it reduplicates – the child's own body, and the persons and things, around him.'[22] The mirror stage, according to Lacan, is to be understood as

> *an identification,* in the full sense that analysis gives to the term: namely the transformation that takes place in the subject when he assumes an image. ...
>
> This jubilant assumption of his specular image by the child at the *infans* stage, still sunk in his motor incapacity and nursling dependence, would seem to exhibit in an exemplary situation the symbolic matrix in which the *I* is precipitated in a primordial form, before it is objectified in the dialectic of identification with the other, and before language restores to it, in the universal, its function as subject.[23]

As the commentators on Lacan, Bice Benvenuto and Roger Kennedy, observe, 'The mirror image inaugurates a new visual and mental experience in the infant's life, since an organised form of himself is seen projected outside, together with the space surrounding him, in the mirror's surface.'[24] Thus the child sees himself within the field. Malcolm Pines, a practising psychoanalyst, has written: 'For Lacan this is the fateful moment when, by identifying with a fiction, the idealised image of himself that he perceives in the mirror, the agency of the ego is cast, the primordial basis of the I that is alienated from the subject.'[25]

In the nine months or so that Newman contemplated his painting, he came to recognise it as a reflection of self which, transformed into the other, provoked a feeling of confrontation. While the initial recognition prompted wonder – 'I realised that I'd made a statement' – there was also a strong sensation of alienation which is repeated for the viewer when he stands before the painting. In not immediately recognising what he had done, however, Newman was no different from any other artist who sets out to communicate something without being able to define exactly what it is. At their most adventurous, artists will often be on the edge between control and uncontrol, trying to extract something new and unexpected. By control, I do not necessarily imply control of the means of production but rather the preconceptualisation of the look and intended meaning of the finished work. If Jackson Pollock was manifestly an exemplar of this practice, Newman, whose work seems so contrastingly classical, structured and premeditated,[26] is no less of one. Newman allied himself to a small number of artists breaking new ground in this way, working intuitively and, in some cases, allegedly out of the unconscious. In a letter to Lester Markel of the *New York Times*, Newman wrote in defence of Clyfford Still: 'Clyfford Still ... belongs to a group of artists who are working at the periphery of known art experiences'.[27]

The unease that Newman must have felt during the course of the period he 'lived with' the painting corresponds to early infantile behaviour. Pines states that while 'there is a stage of joyful recognition and of play with the mirror image in the first year, ... in the second year children withdraw and become "leery" of their images, becoming painfully self-conscious ... and some of that feeling remains with us throughout life, as embarrassment'.[28] If I am self-consciousness it suggests that I can see myself. I am conscious of or have a fantasy of how I appear to others. Jean-Paul Sartre, in his influential treatise, *Being and Nothingness*, published in 1943, portrayed the state of being watched as a threat to the self. In this he was drawing on Hegel's notion of lordship and bondage. For Hegel, recognition is the manifestation of power relations. To be recognised you have to assert your power and superiority over the other but if you do so to the point of annihilating the other, then your superiority remains unrecognised, for the recogniser perishes. Thus for the self to be recognised, he must invest the other with superior power. At the moment of recognition the self becomes slave to the other. Self-consciousness is thus a dialectical state of threatening and being threatened, assertion and submission, gazing and being gazed at.[29] It is that self-consciousness, self-awareness and sense of threat that I feel as I stand before a painting such as *Onement I* and that perhaps Newman felt as he became acquainted with 'the thing' he had made. Or as Newman put it in a statement he published in *Artnews* in 1966: 'Just as I affect the canvas, so does the canvas affect me.'[30]

Pines proposes looking and being looked at as a fundamental process in personality development and in finding out who one is and who one

Girl before a Mirror
Pablo Picasso, 1932
Oil on canvas
162.3 x 130.2 cm
The Museum of Modern
Art, New York. Gift of
Mrs Simon Guggenheim

is not. Picasso's *Girl before a Mirror* (1932), which Newman would have known from visiting the Museum of Modern Art, is in a long tradition of mirror images allegorising the quest for self-knowledge. Here the youthful Marie-Thérèse Walter examines her naked body in the mirror, like a pubescent adolescent, while her double, reflected in the mirror, gazes back intently. The examination is not so much through Marie-Thérèse's gaze but by the extension of her arm to touch the mirror, as though to feel the contours of the body of the other. What she discovers is that the reflected image is not a replica of self but a disconcerting other. It has a face that seems masculine, sometimes interpreted as a death mask, its breasts are differently disposed and coloured. The other takes on an independence from the self. The painting also manifests a subtle example of the power of the other over the self, for while the reflected image gazes intently at the figure before the mirror, the latter, disturbed by what she sees, submissively averts her gaze. The reflected image wins the struggle for mastery over the self while, simultaneously, Marie-Thérèse, looking out of the painting, engages in combat with the viewer. As other commentators have indicated in relation to *Onement I*, Picasso's painting is split down the centre by an orange and blue stripe representing the mirror stand. Picasso's painting is not a source for *Onement I*, at least not a conscious one, but there are interesting echoes.

The examination of self was a topos of Newman's paintings. In 1965 he wrote in the catalogue to his exhibition at the São Paulo Bienal: 'The Fetish and the ornament, blind and mute, impress only those who cannot look at the terror of Self. The self, terrible and constant, is for me the subject matter of painting and sculpture.'[31] For Newman, painting was a painful act of introspection and projection and a struggle for mastery. Lawrence Alloway, who knew Newman well, wrote in the catalogue to the exhibition of *The Stations of the Cross* at the Guggenheim Museum in 1966 that they 'were arrived at through a process of self-recognition'.[32] It is likely that Alloway's statement was derived from something Newman had said in conversation.

Newman was familiar with the writings of Hegel and most likely those of Sartre, for whom the relationship between self and other was a central theme. A translation of *Being and Nothingness*, published in New York by the Philosophical Library in 1956, was in Newman's library. The late date of this translation might suggest that he had not come across Sartre by

1948. However, Existentialism was in the air in the post-war period and Newman might have gained at least second-hand knowledge of it before 1956, perhaps through Harold Rosenberg who showed a keen interest. Whether or not Newman was familiar with Sartre, there is an element of synchronous interest in the examination of self.

Christopher Macann summarises Sartre's theory of the 'Body-for-itself', adumbrated in chapter two of *Being and Nothingness*, as follows: 'I am first and foremost my body. Second it is as a body that the self appears to others. And, finally, my sense of self is largely derived from the way others respond to that body as which I appear to them.'[33] Transposed to Newman's quest for knowledge of the self, he produces an image that depicts the self. In its depiction it becomes the other. It reflects the self back to him. Thus his sense of self is determined by what he sees before him. Finally, it terrifies him because what he perceives is not only an object of power but a state of being split. In a review of the work of Adolph Gottlieb and Rufino Tamayo, Newman wrote:

> Man is a tragic being, and the heart of this tragedy is the metaphysical problem of part and whole. This dichotomy of our nature, from which we can never escape and which because of its nature impels us helplessly to try to resolve it, motivates our struggle for perfection and seals our inevitable doom. For man is one, he is single, he is alone; and yet he belongs, he is part of another. This conflict is the greatest of our tragedies.[34]

For Newman, painting was a quest for wholeness, a search for salvation and reparation in the post-war period of uncertainty and anxiety. In this he strongly echoed the late nineteenth-century debates that declared that the ills of modern society resulted from a lack of a sense of unity, coherence and meaning.[35]

For the artist to launch a painting into the world is an act of birth. Having once been a part of him it is expelled and individuated, assuming its own identity. Thereafter, by mirroring him, the painting has a determining effect on the artist's identity. Although it was not Newman's first painting, he described *Onement I* as 'the beginning of my present life', thus acknowledging not only that the painting was him (painting = my life) but that it represented a birth. From that moment on he found a metaphor for the state of separation in the vertical 'zips' and, for the remainder of his life, he struggled with the search to regain a state of wholeness. The conflict that Newman describes and underwent was in effect a process of mourning the loss of wholeness and an attempt to recover the lost object, that from which he had been separated.[36]

The concept of wholeness is one that has concerned philosophers and religious commentators for centuries but it has been of particular concern to writers in the twentieth century. Martin Heidegger, the German philosopher, was perhaps one of the most influential in this field. He distinguished between authentic and inauthentic moments. As Dermot Moran explains, '*Authentic* moments are those in which we are most at home with ourselves, at one with ourselves'. That is, we experience things personally and wholeheartedly rather than indirectly. 'Being authentic is a kind of potential-to-be whole: humans have the urge to get their lives together, to collect themselves, to gather themselves into wholeness.'[37] For Heidegger the quest is to recover a sense of being, of *Dasein*, of 'is-there'. The problem, according to Heidegger, is that *Dasein* is essentially always unfinished because it ends in death. The experience of other people's death is inauthentic because it is not a first-person experience: first-person, conscious experience of death is impossible, thus *Dasein* is a state of incompleteness.

The notion of death as the only way of attaining wholeness underpinned Sigmund Freud's essay 'Beyond the Pleasure Principle', first published in 1920, seven years before Heidegger's *Being and Time*. Freud maintained – and this issue continues to be debated by psychoanalytical theorists – that life is controlled by an overriding death instinct: that the self-preservation instinct is a manifestation of an urge for wholeness and that wholeness can only come to fruition through organic death. Freud proposes that 'the goal of life' is to attain 'a state of things' which must 'be an *old* state of things, an initial state from which the living entity has at one time or other departed and to which it is striving to return by the circuitous paths along which development leads'.[38] The aim of life, according to Freud, is a return to the inanimate state that exists before life. Man is governed by '*an urge inherent in organic life to restore an earlier state of things*' (his italics).[39]

What Freud proposes, echoing Nietzsche,[40] is essentially that wholeness, or 'completion' to use his term, involves a return to a

primordial, or perhaps pre-primordial, state of being. There is an
interesting parallel between this and Newman's writings about
indigenous art. Newman maintained that present-day artists should not
be distinguished from their earliest forebears. His interpretation of the
latter's art and actions are a reflection of his own interests. 'We have come
to realise that these sculptors were interested in the elemental mystery
of life,' he writes about pre-Columbian sculptors. 'We today are still
concerned with the same problem'.[41] Newman argued that far from being
primitive, the art of the ancient Oceanic and Indian cultures was highly
sophisticated. The aim of the present-day artist was 'to discover the
original impulse', to return to 'the artist's prime function' which was to be
'preoccupied with the creation of gods, with the expression of forces, with
numinous beings' that had been the concern of the first artists.[42] Art was
a means to return to a primordial state of being. As he put it in an article
titled 'The First Man Was an Artist': 'What is the raison d'être, what is the
explanation of the seemingly insane drive of man to be a painter and poet
if it is not an act of defiance against man's fall and an assertion that he
return to the Adam of the Garden of Eden?'[43] But it is an act of futility.
A return to the Adam of the Garden of Eden is a return to a state of
wholeness, to the earliest stage of mankind before man had learnt to
differentiate himself from woman and before the expulsion; in other
words before the split. In *Onement I* and subsequent works Newman
enacts the moment of the loss of wholeness, the moment when the first
man made the first mark, which was, Newman fantasised, a stick drawn
through the mud, an act of creation but also destruction that he repeats
throughout the remainder of his life.[44]

* * *

I am standing in front of *Onement I*. I see a maroon field (Indian red) split
by an orange vertical stripe (cadmium red light). The field has an uneven,
relatively thin paint film; the orange stripe has a thick impasto and is
painted onto and overlaps a piece of masking tape. It is a searing orange,
a somewhat painful interjection into a field of doleful colour. It stands
proud, a form against a ground, and in this it is almost, although not quite,
unique in Newman's oeuvre. I look at the painting and stare into its
blankness. I could walk on because I have seen all there is to see but

I linger in the hope that it will reveal something more. As I continue to look I become aware of myself in the act of looking. The blankness and the singularity of the image refer me back to myself. The vertical band reminds me of my own verticality and I begin to connect myself to the painting. I start to feel self-conscious and to sense my own presence in the room. I look at the object in front of me and it provokes a feeling of discomfort, as though I am looking into a mirror.

Repetition is the key to Newman. With the exception of the few works with horizontal stripes, all of Newman's subsequent work returned to the same motif albeit in different formats. For Freud, repetition is a compulsive aspect of human behaviour and represents a search for mastery.

> What appears in a tiny minority of human individuals as an untiring impulsion towards further perfection can easily be understood as a result of the instinctual repression upon which is based all that is most precious in human civilisation. The repressed instinct never ceases to strive for complete satisfaction, which would consist in the repetition of a primary experience of satisfaction. ... [It] is the difference in amount between the pleasure of satisfaction which is *demanded* and that which is actually *achieved* that provides the driving factor which will permit of no halting at any position attained.[45]

Repetition, Freud argues, is a manifestation of infantile behaviour and, in an adult, signifies an unconscious desire to return to an earlier state (hence the link with Newman's avowed association with the earliest artists). It is also fundamental to psychoanalytic treatment and to the concept of trauma.

Trauma manifests itself not at the time of a particular event but when that event is recalled. Freud termed this process *Nachträglichkeit*, often understood as deferred action. Freud maintained that the human being 'revises past events at a later date and that it is this revision that invests them with efficacy or pathogenic force'. As he wrote to Wilhelm Fliess on 6 December 1896: 'I am working on the assumption that our psychical mechanism has come into being by a process of stratification: the material present in the form of memory-traces being subjected from

time to time to a *re-arrangement* in accordance with fresh circumstances –
to a *re-transcription*.'[46] Theoretically trauma can be relieved, if not cured,
by what psychoanalysts calls abreaction, the relief of anxiety by the
expression and release of a previously repressed emotion. In the course
of therapy the patient returns repeatedly to the traumatic event to
relive the experience and the emotional reaction in changing ways.
The experience is revised and rearranged according to the circumstances
(physical or psychical) in which he finds himself. This process is
similar to Newman's process of painting, returning each time to the
originary impulse to make and recasting it in a different form. As he
stated to Dorothy Gees Seckler: 'I start each painting as if I had never
painted before.'[47]

The notion of art as a therapeutic activity is a commonplace. In *The
Birth of Tragedy* Nietzsche writes: '*art* approaches as a saving sorceress
with the power to heal. Art alone can re-direct those repulsive thoughts
about the terrible or absurd nature of existence into representations with
which man can live; these representations are the *sublime*, where the
terrible is tamed by artistic means' (his italics).[48] Newman was highly
critical of Nietzsche but there is no doubt but that some of his ideas
resurface in Newman's writings and practice.

So what traumas might Newman have been addressing in his art?
In the first instance, as a Jew who lived through the Second World War,
he was deeply affected by the news of the death camps, although he
remained fairly silent on the issue. Moreover, as an American he had
a strong sense of the enormity (perhaps also guilt) of the dropping of the
atom bomb. In 'Surrealism and the War' Newman refers directly to the
'German atrocities', stating: 'The sadism in those pictures [of German
atrocities], the horror and the pathos are around us.'[49] In 'A New Sense
of Fate' he referred to the bombing of Hiroshima:

> The war the surrealists predicted has robbed us of our hidden terror,
> as terror can exist only if the forces of tragedy are unknown. We now
> know the terror to expect. Hiroshima showed it to us. We are no
> longer, then, in the face of a mystery. After all, wasn't it an American
> boy who did it? The terror has indeed become as real as life. What
> we have now is a tragic rather than a terrifying situation.[50]

The event has taken place and the original experience of terror, when recalled, is transformed into tragedy, a situation to be replayed and reflected upon. It is, in effect, traumatic.

Thomas Hess recounts that Newman linked the invented word 'onement' to 'at-onement', signifying the process of atonement as a way of regaining a state of wholeness, being at one.[51] Atonement is of course an important aspect of Judaism and one might speculate that *Onement I* is an expression of the feelings of guilt often felt by Jewish survivors of the Holocaust.[52] Newman refers repeatedly in his writings to the tragic state in which his contemporaries find themselves and the state of terror in which they live. Here was a man whose writings consistently express the condition of trauma. Up until *Onement I* all Newman's paintings concerned biblical and human creation represented in biomorphic forms. In the aftermath of war Newman realised that creation was no longer an innocent or sexual subject and that lyricism was not simply distasteful but somehow untruthful. His abandonment of this lyric mode for something more austere embodies T.W. Adorno's celebrated statement that 'to write lyric poetry after Auschwitz is barbaric' but that in art alone suffering can find its own voice and consolation.[53] Art was thus an act of defiance against silence as well as an expression of grief. The pre-eminent subject in the post-war era was death, what Newman termed 'the greatest of all life's mysteries'.[54] If *Onement I* was an act of birth it also embodied the potential for death for the act of creation implies a split, the loss of wholeness. In the book of Genesis this is symbolised by the division of the land from the sea, by the differentiation of night from day and by the birth of Eve from Adam's rib. In the act of human birth the infant is parted from the mother, the severing of the umbilical chord being the physical manifestation of what will be the ongoing psychological process of individuation and separation finally achieved in the death of the parent who, paradoxically, at exactly that moment is reincorporated psychically by the child, thus achieving, once again, a certain state of wholeness. Birth is therefore a moment of loss, an act of splitting, death a moment of wholeness, or reunification. Life is thus a quest to recover that wholeness, or what Julia Kristeva calls 'the lost object'.[55] *Onement I* is emblematic of a split and represents, almost literally, an attempt to repair it, to bandage it over with a piece of masking tape.

There is no concrete evidence that Newman felt that the making of

Onement I was either an expression of trauma or itself a traumatic act, but the fact that he told Sylvester that it 'was affecting me' indicates some kind of assault on the senses. Credibility is lent to this interpretation by Newman's retrospective remarks on the making of the black on black *Abraham* of the following year: 'The terror of it was intense ... I call it terror. It's more than anxiety.'[56] Terror, when recollected, is traumatic. Trauma is defined as

> An event in the subject's life defined by its intensity, by the subject's incapacity to respond adequately to it, and by the upheaval and long-lasting effects that it brings about in the physical organisation. In economic terms, the trauma is characterised by an influx of excitations that is excessive by the standard of the subject's tolerance and capacity to master such excitations and work them out physically.[57]

It seems to me that Newman's compulsion to repeat the same gesture again and again over the next twenty years is a strong indication of a disturbance or an 'upheaval' and a desire for mastery. While some commentators see this as a desire for mastery over language, that is only a partial explanation. Newman was not interested in the language of painting as an end in itself but as a means to express the verbally inexpressible, a means to recover something lost: on one level the losses arising from the Second World War and the Holocaust; on another level a sense of wholeness, contact with the primal or, in Heidegger's terms, his sense of being. It is significant that within a year of making *Onement I* Newman ceased to write articles. It was as though words were an inadequate vehicle for the expression of his ideas, or the recovery of the loss, and that painting represented the only means to do so. For Newman, painting was a pre-verbal language of primal marks, 'yells of awe and anger'.[58] More than simply a desire for mastery of language, the act of repetition manifests an unconscious desire to come to terms with or overcome a disturbance; it is an act of redemption. He may not realise why he is engaged with repetition, but it is a compulsive act, part of the process of mourning.

For Kristeva, repetition is a manifestation of depression which arises during the process of mourning. Depressive speech is 'repetitive, monotonous, or empty of meaning'. She continues: 'Signs are arbitrary because language starts with a *negation (Verneinung)* of loss, along with the depression occasioned by mourning. "I have lost an essential object that happens to be, in the final analysis, my mother," is what the speaking being seems to be saying. "But no, I have found her again in signs, or rather since I consent to lose her I have not lost her (that is the negation), I can recover her in language".'[59] Mourning, according to Kristeva, 'drives out negation and revives the memory of signs by drawing them out of their signifying neutrality. It loads them with affects, and this results in making them ambiguous, repetitive, or simply alliterative, musical or sometimes nonsensical'. This is but another means to search for a new way of expressing the loss, of 'capturing the unnameable'.[60] For Freud, as for Kristeva, death is not representable in the unconscious. 'It is imprinted there ... by spacings, blanks, discontinuities, or destruction of representation',[61] a description appropriate to the paintings of Newman.

Beyond the impact of the Holocaust and the dropping of the bomb – and without attempting to psychoanalyse Newman through the limited biographical information we have – within Newman's life there were very specific moments that might be interpreted as the cause of traumatic experience and which, I propose, he unconsciously abreacted through the process of painting. The first was the creation of *Onement I*, the recognition of the self as other, which only took on its true meaning retrospectively by the repetition of the motif.[62] Had Newman returned to painting in the style of earlier works the significance of this painting would, I think, pale. The second was the death of his father, after which he painted *Abraham* (1949); the third was his heart attack which engendered *Outcry* (1958) and *The Stations of the Cross*; the fourth was the death of his brother George, memorialised in *Shining Forth (to George)* (1961); and the fifth was the death of his mother, commemorated in *Anna's Light* (1968).

To take *The Stations of the Cross* as an example; Newman wrote a text to accompany the exhibition at the Guggenheim in which he explains why he subtitled the exhibition '*Lema Sabachthani*'.[63] '*Lema Sabachthani* – why? Why did you forsake me? Why forsake me? To what purpose? Why?' The repetitive structure of these questions is not insignificant. With each question Newman seems to be addressing the same point in a modified way. To use Freud's term, he re-transcribes it. Newman concludes: 'The question has no answer', just as re-living the traumatic experience can never provide an answer, simply an accommodation through repeated abreaction. When Newman embarked on the *Stations* he had not conceived of a series. The first two were executed in 1958, following his heart attack in November 1957. The second two were painted in 1960. 'It was after the fourth that he realised the number and meaning of the work on which he was engaged', Alloway wrote.[64] There could never be a better example of deferred action.

The first four paintings in the group are the most closely resembling. The structure of the left side of each is exactly similar except that the first two are painted in Magna and the second two in oil. The right sides present alternatives where the key elements occur at approximately the same point on the canvas. Thus the firm, definable left edges of the 'zips' are the same distance from the right edge of the canvas. It is significant, therefore, that Newman, if Alloway is to be believed, realised the meaning of his actions only after repeating the first work three times. Repetition provided him with meaning. In fact all the *Stations* start out the same way. The left edge, whether unpainted or not, has an element more or less the same width. The group is a continuous rehearsal of the same theme.

Newman interpreted Christ's walk up the Via Dolorosa as a metaphor for his own suffering and Christ's questioning of God as a metaphor for Newman's own sense of injustice. It is not, as Alloway confirms, a series of variations on a theme, but 'a continuous agony. ... [They] have to be experienced as a unit of fourteen continuous parts. ... He regards the group as a cry.'[65] The fact that George died during the course of the making of the series, that he was memorialised in a similarly black and unprimed canvas painting and that the series took eight years to complete, suggests that the *Stations* had a strong therapeutic function.

The act of repetition, however, is not simply a means to a therapeutic end or to an understanding of trauma. Freud also identified it as a cause of the uncanny. In his celebrated essay of 1919, Freud defines the uncanny as something which is familiar, often from childhood, and has remained secret or repressed but which unexpectedly returns. Mirror reflections and the double are frequently associated with the uncanny. Freud explains that while the double was regarded in earlier cultures as 'insurance against destruction of the ego', it soon became 'the uncanny harbinger of death'.[66] Otto Rank, in *The Double*, first published in 1914, and to which Freud has recourse in his essay on the uncanny, provides examples in literature where the absence of the double or the extinction of the double leads to the death of the self. According to Freud, under certain conditions the double becomes something foreign and an object of dread, but as long as it is there it confirms the existence of the self.

In looking at Newman's paintings – *Uriel*, for example – the vertical 'zips' remind me of my existence by mirroring my verticality at the edge of a vast aqua field. The black vertical is isolated from the earth colour to which it is related and the earth colour itself is cleaved apart by a shaft of white. Wholeness is lost and existence is precarious. The frailty of the edges of the 'zips' suggests that engulfment, the expansion of the two areas of aqua, is a distinct possibility, leading to annihilation. This is the characteristic of the sublime described by Edmund Burke: 'whilst we contemplate so vast an object', he wrote, 'under the arm, as it were of an almighty power, and invested upon every side with omnipresence, we shrink into the minuteness of our own nature, and are, in a manner annihilated before him.'[67] As I contemplate *Uriel* I am reminded of my mortality in the same way that Marie-Thérèse is before the mirror. I have an uncanny experience of foreseeing my death.

In *The Stations of the Cross*, the series begins with what Barbara Reise graphically described as 'a skinny unprimed zip' in the first painting 'screech[ing] up and down a blackboard of dry-brushed edges', and ends with 'the complete release in the annihilation of the right zone into the soft whiteness of the last step.'[68] The elimination of the double, the 'zip', in the final painting suggests extinction. All ruggedness and imperfection associated with the sublime is eliminated. The abject condition of the body under stress, metaphorised in the biblical narrative and in the messy, at times almost faecal, brushwork, and the oil bleeds, the occurrence of which Newman would surely have anticipated in many of the *Stations*, is veiled in a white shroud. Yet, the *Stations* do not embody a progression in a narrative sense. In fact, quite the opposite. By the act of repetition Newman creates a sense of a frozen moment, a suspended narrative that repeats itself in various guises. Each painting recalls the previous ones, is the double of another and evokes a sense of the uncanny.[69]

When I am confronted by a group of Newman paintings a feeling of the uncanny will often arise. This is not simply because I see in the painting an echo of my own body or because I project myself onto the painting as though it were a mirror, but because each painting recalls in some way the previous one. As you look at each new painting you feel as though you are confronted by something strangely new but oddly familiar. Thomas Hess observed: 'In each Newman painting, there are years of other Newmans, each inflecting the other, quietly, remorselessly.'[70]

Although not strictly relevant to my argument it is worth taking a moment to consider whether Newman had any interest in psychoanalytic ideas. There was a lot of discussion about psychoanalysis in the late 1930s and 1940s and it would have been impossible for him to have been untouched by that.[71] Surrealism had made a big impact in New York, not least because a number of European artists and writers sought refuge from Fascism across the Atlantic. Newman himself was a great admirer of Miró. Even before that there was widespread interest in the writings of Freud and Jung that Newman would not have been able to avoid. Jung's 'modern man' theory, first published in an English translation in 1933, is interestingly echoed in Newman's writings. 'Modern Man', Jung writes,

> is ... the man who stands upon a peak, or at the very edge of the world, the abyss of the future before him. ... Indeed he is completely modern only when he has come to the very edge of the world ... acknowledging that he stands before a void out of which all things may grow.[72]

Newman would have had a sympathy for Jung's view that 'Science has destroyed even the refuge of inner life. What was once a sheltering haven has become a place of terror'.[73] Writing about what he called 'original man', and associating himself with the former's primordial condition, Newman declared: 'Original man, shouting his consonants, did so in yells of awe and anger at his tragic state, at his own self-awareness and at his own helplessness before the void.'[74] This statement, written in 1947, in the full knowledge of the impact of the Nazi concentration camps and the nuclear attacks on Japan, must surely indicate a knowledge of Jung. The fact that Newman's friend and colleague Jackson Pollock underwent a Jungian psychotherapy and that John Graham, the Russian emigré artist who wrote on 'primitive' art and was known to Newman, was also a Jung aficionado, makes it likely that Newman was well aware of psychoanalytic ideas. Finally, Jung's statement that 'Nothing goes to show that primitive man thinks, feels, or perceives in a way that fundamentally differs from ours' is echoed many times in Newman's writings.[75] As for Freud, Newman possessed a copy of his *An Outline of Psychoanalysis*, published in 1949 by W.W. Norton and Co. Of course, this does not prove that Newman read the book or, even if he did, when that might have been. However, the fact that he owned it increases the likelihood that he was aware of basic psychoanalytic thinking.

Thus far I have used psychoanalytic models as a means to understand certain givens within Newman's work: in particular, division and repetition. Repetition is, of course, a characteristic of the work of many artists from Mondrian through to the Minimalists. However, I have been careful not to refer to Newman's work or groups of work as series, because any attempt to link it to seriality would, in my view, be erroneous. Seriality has a relationship to mass-production and of course to artists of the succeeding generation such as Donald Judd and Andy Warhol. Unlike Newman, their work was based on serial progression or variation and grids, using such means to disguise or dispense with personal expression to the extent that their work was frequently executed by other hands. Art was the product of a manufacturing ethos and, in the case of Judd, process. As a writer and an artist, Newman was concerned to reveal himself. Repetition in Newman has more to do with obsession, in the same way that Picasso repeatedly returned to the same subjects in an obsessive manner. Both artists sought some kind of mastery, whether over language, personal feelings, objects, precursors or contemporaries. Where Picasso had a rivalry with Rembrandt, Manet, Matisse or Braque, Newman pitted himself against Mondrian, Rothko and Still.

Newman did not consciously paint in a way informed by psychoanalytic thinking. I doubt that he would have conceived of the act of making art as a process of therapy. But given what we know about him and his sympathies, unless his writings of the 1940s are nothing but empty rhetoric and bluster, we can say that he was deeply affected by world events and by the events of his own life and that through his art he sought to reveal and master his feelings about them. Psychoanalytic models can help us to come to a more profound understanding of why an art of such limited means can have such potential for meaning.

* * *

I am standing in front of *Onement I.* I see a maroon field (Indian red) split by an orange vertical stripe (cadmium red light). The field has an uneven, relatively thin paint film; the orange stripe has a thick impasto and is painted onto and overlaps a piece of masking tape. It is a searing orange, a somewhat painful interjection into a field of doleful colour. It stands proud, a form against a ground, and in this it is almost, although not quite, unique in Newman's oeuvre. I look at the painting and stare into its blankness. I could walk on because I have seen all there is to see but I linger in the hope that it will reveal something more. As I continue to look I become aware of myself in the act of looking. The blankness and the singularity of the image refer me back to myself. The vertical band reminds me of my own verticality and I begin to connect myself to the painting. I start to feel self-conscious and to sense my own presence in the room. I look at the object in front of me and it provokes a feeling of discomfort, as though I am looking into a mirror.

From an early date writers have suggested phenomenological readings of Newman's paintings. In an article of 1958, E.C. Goossen referred to Monet's *Nymphéas* as a precedent for Newman's paintings. He considered in respect of the Monets that 'Their whole impact, their whole meaning perhaps, depends precisely on the *absence* of the figure. ... The presence of the figure would define the scale of the picture from the *inside* in terms of the proportion of the human body, and the picture's scale depends upon its relation to the human body of the spectator *outside*'. The picture becomes 'a *thing* ... It is no longer a window to a world, but *the* world, immanent and autonomous. ... The human figure was forced out of the picture to rejoin its alter egos, the artist and the spectator' (his italics).[76] Photographs of Newman's paintings in his exhibition at Bennington College, Vermont, in 1958, for the catalogue of which Goossen wrote an essay, show Goossen and an unidentified woman standing in front of *Vir Heroicus Sublimis*, as though enacting Goossen's proposition that scale is determined in relation to the human body.[77]

Kaprow also wrote in phenomenological terms when describing his response to *Vir Heroicus Sublimis*:

> The stops [as Kaprow termed the 'zips'] ... submerge and drown in
> the vast sea of intense red, neither voids nor solids. We may guess
> that it is *ourselves*, the viewers, who are assigned the role of 'objects',

and the painting is the still 'ground' in relation to which we move and feel. In both a metaphorical and literal sense, we are the imagery of an art which deeply involves the human being. [78]

Even if Newman had not read any phenomenological texts, others around him had. Phenomenology is an attempt to discover the truth through a 'reduction' to the primary experience without the filter of a priori metaphysical premises, the distortions of folk assumptions and scientific knowledge. It emphasises personal, unadulterated experience of the object, getting 'back to the things themselves' as Edmund Husserl, a pioneer of this philosophical outlook, put it, and rejects the Cartesian separation between mind and body. For Maurice Merleau-Ponty, 'the world is not what I think, but what I live through'.[79] Just as Newman advocated a return to a primordial state, so phenomenologists urged a return to 'a presuppositionless science of consciousness'.[80] There is a parallel here with Newman's desire to start painting 'from scratch'[81] and with his statement in an interview with Dorothy Gees Seckler: 'The fact is, I am an intuitive painter, a direct painter. I have never

E.C. Goossen and an unidentified woman in front of *Vir Heroicus Sublimis* (1950–51), Bennington College, Vermont, 1958

worked from sketches, never planned a painting, never "thought out" a painting. I start each painting as if I had never painted before. I present no dogma, no system, no demonstrations.'[82] Newman's emphasis here on the separateness of each work, begun as though no previous painting existed, and elsewhere on painting as a means to making statements about the human condition, echo Husserl's belief that the universal is seen in the individual. As Moran writes: 'The move from the individual intuition to the grasp of the universal is a move to grasp the essence', which Husserl called eidetic intuition.[83] For Husserl it was important to be able to reclaim our infantile experiences of objects, returning to 'an original becoming acquainted',[84] relearning how to see. Newman's affinity for the art of indigenous cultures could be interpreted as a step in this direction. His reduction to a basic grammar of painting could be another: the trace of a 'stick through the mud', the first gesture, a return to the origin.

If phenomenologists reject the separation of mind and body they place particular emphasis on the gaining of knowledge through bodily experience. Merleau-Ponty wrote that 'we perceive the world through our body' and concluded that he 'could not grasp the unity of the object without the mediation of bodily experience'.[85] When I look at a particularly wide painting – *Vir Heroicus Sublimis*, for example – I cannot grasp its totality from one spot, particularly if I take Newman's advice and look at it 'from a short distance'.[86] I am obliged to walk along the painting. If I am close enough, even turning my head from side to side will not give me the full experience of the work. Standing facing the centre, at a distance of about ten feet, I have a peripheral awareness of the white 'zip' on the far right but I cannot see the red 'zip' closer to me on the far left. The only way to experience the painting is to move along it and experience it from different positions and from each position my experience is altered. In fact the experience as a totality is cumulative because from wherever I view it, I bring to my present perception the experience of viewing it from another position. And as I do so, those elements that previously stood out now merge back into the field: figure and ground become interchangeable. The general proposition of the variable status of figure and ground was remarked upon by Sartre in *Being and Nothingness*: 'No one object, no group of objects is especially designed to be organised as specifically either ground or figure: all depends on the direction of my attention.'[87] The lack of differentiation between figure and ground, or rather the elimination of any such relationship in Newman's paintings, is apparent from very soon after the making of *Onement I* and is particularly clear in paintings where there are no narrow 'zips' but just broad bands of colour. Such works as *Voice of Fire*, *White and Hot* and *Now II*, all of 1967, and *Who's Afraid of Red Yellow and Blue IV* of 1969–70 exemplify this non-hierarchical relationship between colour fields. Even in *Chartres*, one of Newman's triangular works, the blue vertical bands do not project or recede but remain resolutely in the same plane as the broad areas of colour. In an interview with Emile de Antonio, Newman put this point emphatically: 'I feel that my zip does not divide my paintings. I feel it does the exact opposite. It does not cut the format in half or in whatever parts, but it does the exact opposite: it unites the thing. It creates a totality, and in this regard I feel very, very separate, let's say, from other mental views, the so-called stripes.'[88] Newman was concerned to construct a delicate equilibrium between colours and tones, not to create projections and recessions. Flatness was important. The paintings are to that extent non-hierarchical.

If I move even closer to the surface of *Vir Heroicus Sublimis* I detect that the red field is not a smooth surface but is a little cloudy. I can also see that there is a considerable amount of overpainting, that there are areas of bleed between one colour and another, that the edges of the 'zips' break down and are frayed in places, and that some 'zips' seem to be in a state of continual transformation from one tone to another. Having walked from side to side, if I return to the centre and gaze directly in front of me I look into a red void bounded by the white and red 'zips' either side of the centre. I project myself against the void and become the embodiment of a central 'zip'. I am aware of my body as a presence before the painting. In a Sartrean sense this is a space in which I can act.

Merleau-Ponty took this further. For him human beings and objects do not simply take up space but inhabit it and there is a mutuality and interrelatedness between them, between self and other. While the subject may gaze at the object, the object may gaze back. Kaprow noted this when he wrote: 'Being impenetrable, the red returns our penetrating stare reciprocally.'[89] For Merleau-Ponty every object is a mirror. 'To look at an object is to inhabit it, and from this habitation to grasp all things in terms of the aspect which they present to it.'[90] The gaze migrates around a room to every object and, in inhabiting it, sees all objects from different angles

Overleaf: Barnett Newman and an unidentified woman with *Cathedra* (1951) in Newman's Front Street studio, 1958. Photograph by Peter A. Juley

providing a cumulative 360 degree understanding for the perceiving subject. If I transpose this to the experience of looking at a Newman, the information I gain about my body from standing in front of, for example, *Anna's Light*, can never be complete because I cannot see behind me. Thus I cannot understand fully the relationship between subject and object. If in addition, however, I experience *Anna's Light* with a body interposed between mine and the painting, I can see the relationship of that body to the painting, the painting's relationship to that body and the full impact they have on each other. I do this through projection, or 'inhabiting', and can add this to my isolated experience of the painting.

In some respects the importance of the physical relationship between the viewer and the painting is increased in Newman's later works where the absence of any narrow 'zips' splitting the field removes any visual measure of scale. This absence obliges the viewer to project himself against the canvas to determine his relationship to it, to measure its extent and to assert his presence. It is a movement of to and fro, of projection and retraction, of independence and absorption. As Alex Potts maintains, in his later writings Merleau-Ponty conceives of seeing as 'a symbiosis, not between something seeing and something seen, but between an inside and an outside, the boundaries of which are constantly shifting. The dynamic is one of enveloping and being enveloped and of encroaching and being encroached upon, not of looking and being looked at.'[91]

The photograph of the exhibition at Bennington, and indeed other photographs of Newman standing or sitting in front of his paintings are key texts. Reading Newman's writings there seems little doubt but that he was a controlling person. Few people were permitted entry to his studio and it is likely that whenever a photographer came Newman would have had a controlling hand in the photographs taken. The shot of him and an unidentified woman standing in front of *Cathedra*, published in Rosenberg's monograph,[92] must have been carefully posed (see pp. 32–33). Here we see both bodies, viewed from behind, flanking a strong white 'zip' located just left of centre. There could be no clearer indication that Newman regarded the 'zip' motif as having a direct relationship to the body and that the body was integral to an understanding of the painting. Without it there would be no indication of scale, no sense of the human and no sense of the relationship of the painting to the surrounding space.

Barnett Newman at Betty Parsons Gallery, New York, 1951. The paintings seen are (left to right) *Onement III*, *Covenant*, *Horizon Light* (hung vertically) and *The Promise*. Double-exposed photograph by Aaron Siskind

The male and female act as surrogate 'zips' and, in characteristic Newman
fashion, they are not placed symmetrically but rather to maintain the
essentially right-sided balance of the work which, without the presence of
people, is established by the fainter 'zip' on the right. Other photographs
are similarly informative. For example, in Aaron Siskind's of Newman at
his 1951 exhibition at Betty Parsons, Newman appears as a vertical
interruption in the plane of the doorway, echoing the paintings on view.
In Hans Namuth's photograph at the same exhibition, Newman stands in
another doorway, his body bifurcated, cut off in an uncanny reprise of the
cropping of the right hand 'zip' of *Eve*. Namuth's rather crass but revealing
double exposure of Newman standing before *Vir Heroicus Sublimis* is a
more literal statement of the relationship of body to 'zip'.[93]

In his interview with David Sylvester, Newman stated:

> One thing I am involved in about painting is that the painting
> should give man a sense of place: that he knows he's there, so he's
> aware of himself. In that sense he relates to me when I made the
> painting because in that sense I was there. And one of the nicest
> things that anybody ever said about my work is when you yourself
> said that standing in front of my paintings you had a sense of your
> own scale. This is what I think you meant, and this is what I have
> tried to do: that the onlooker in front of my painting knows he's
> there. To me the sense of place not only has a mystery but has that
> sense of metaphysical fact. ... I hope that my painting has the impact
> of giving someone, as it did me, the feeling of his own totality, of his
> own separateness, of his own individuality, and at the same time of
> his connection to others, who are also separate.[94]

There is a dynamic of being within and being without.

This is a clear statement of an interest in the concerns of
phenomenology even if they may only have been intuited: the
interconnectedness and simultaneous separation of self and other, the
emphasis on the physical experience of standing before the painting, on
the awareness of being 'there'. Newman rejected the idea that the work of
art was just another object in the world:

> One of the things that I feel I've done [if I've done] something at all
> is that I have removed the emphasis on a painting as an object. After
> all, I was the one who invented the title Subjects of the Artist for the
> school some of us ran on Eighth Street in 1948–49. At the same time
> that does not mean that I'm ignorant of the fact that the painting
> inevitably is a physical object, and today there is an emphasis in
> painting on creating new kinds of objects ... I'm trying to make
> a distinction between an aesthetic object and a work of art. In this
> regard, I think of my painting as an object, but only as an object in
> a grammatical construction. ... The empty canvas is a grammatical
> object – a predicate. I am the subject who paints it. The process of
> painting is the verb. The finished painting is the entire sentence,
> and that's what I'm involved in. ... I'm not interested in adding to

the objects that exist in the world. I want my painting to separate
itself from every object and every art object that exists.[95]

Although he was not interested in the work of art as an object *qua* object,
the fact that he made such works as *The Wild* and *Here III* indicates
that the work of art as a confrontational object occupying space had
resonance for him. 'Scale', as Newman said to Sylvester, 'is a felt thing'.[96]
It was something that could be physically experienced only in the
presence of the object and in the present moment, through the body.
In talking about *The Wild* Newman drew a parallel with his fantasy of
what it might be like to see the tundra. He told Andrew Hudson: 'That is
why in my mind's eye I have always been fascinated by the tundra, where
the feeling of space involves all four horizons.'[97] The phenomenological
360-degree view is invoked.

   As early as 1949 Newman articulated his interest in the congruity of
space and time. In an article about the Miamisburg mounds Newman
described how his experience was not one of looking at the mounds but
of 'looking out as if inside a picture rather than outside contemplating
any specific nature'. Newman thus perceived them through his body.
The 'sensation' he recorded was not one of space but of time, 'not the *sense*
of time but the physical *sensation* of time' (his italics).[98] Newman here
refers to a kinaesthetic process where the body becomes one with the
object or, to use Merleau-Ponty's words, 'inhabits' it. This experience
twenty months after painting *Onement I*, about one year after he 'accepted'
it as a painting, perhaps overtly expressed something he had begun to feel
when confronted with his paintings. It was to underpin Newman's
painting from 1948 until his death.

   * * *

I began this essay by confessing my difficulty in understanding Newman
and in determining an approach to interpreting his art. One of the
strengths of his painting is its susceptibility to varying approaches, be
they structuralist, mystical, formalist, psychoanalytic, phenomenological
or any other. Newman's work is impenetrable but it is that very
impenetrability that provides the clue. The painter stands before the
canvas and projects his thoughts and feelings onto it such that it becomes

an extension or a reflection of him. Newman rejected the concept of the painting as a window on the world. In their resolute flatness his paintings refute the sense of penetration that such a notion might embody. Rather he stood before them and sensed his own presence while contemplating his 'other'. The emphatic signatures on the front face of many of the paintings merely confirm such a reading. He could have signed them on the back like Rothko and Still, but he made a conscious decision to sign the front. While the presence of the signature might be interpreted by some as confirmation of the status of the paintings as object, it has a distinct metaphorical value. *Not There – Here* is one of his titles, as if to fix his presence and to request or command attention. 'Look at me', or as Bruce Nauman memorably put it in a work of 1973: 'Pay attention'. It is a declaration of the immediate, the here and now, a temporal and spatial statement. Be aware of your presence in space and time as I am when I paint the work. As Newman put it to Sylvester: 'I hope that my painting has the impact of giving someone, as it did me, the feeling of his own totality, of his own separateness, of his own individuality, and at the same time of his connection to others, who are also separate.'

Notes

1. '... in my opinion Newman is the most difficult artist I can name.' Yve-Alain Bois, 'Here to There and Back', *Artforum*, vol.40, no.7, March 2002, p.106. In this article Bois outlines the history of the critical reception of Newman.

2. Jean-François Lyotard, 'Newman: the Instant' in Andrew Benjamin (ed.), *The Lyotard Reader*, Oxford 1989, p.242

3. Ibid., p.241

4. Donald Judd, 'Barnett Newman', *Studio International*, February 1970, pp.66–9. This piece was originally written for *Das Kunstwerk* but they did not publish it.

5. Allen Kaprow, 'Impurity', *Artnews*, January 1963, p.55

6. Letter from Barbara Reise to Barnett Newman, 15 March 1966, Tate Archive

7. Harold Rosenberg, 'The Art World. Meaning in Abstract Art', *New Yorker*, 1 January 1972, p.46

8. Peter Plagens, 'Zip: Another Magazine Article on Barnett Newman', *Art in America*, November 1971, p.63; Barbara Rose, 'The Primacy of Color', *Art International*, May 1964, p.26

9. Barnett Newman, 'Painting and Prose/Frankenstein' in John P. O'Neill (ed.), *Barnett Newman Selected Writings and Interviews*, Berkeley and Los Angeles 1992, p.87 (hereafter referred to as *Selected Writings*)

10. 'The Plasmic Image' in *Selected Writings*, p.155

11. 'The Problem of Subject Matter' in *Selected Writings*, p.80

12. 'The Plasmic Image' in *Selected Writings*, p.155

13. Ann Temkin has shown that apart from some of his earliest known works, Newman did not ascribe titles to his paintings until 1958 and then did so retrospectively. This does not mean, however, that Newman did not think of his paintings at the time of their making in terms alluded to by the titles he subsequently ascribed to them, merely that, as Temkin states, the fashion in the early 1950s was to call works 'untitled'. 'Barnett Newman on Exhibition' in Ann Temkin (ed.), *Barnett Newman*, exhibition catalogue, Philadelphia Museum of Art, Philadelphia 2002, p.51

14. 'For Impassioned Criticism' in *Selected Writings*, p.131

15. See Armin Zweite, *Barnett Newman. Paintings. Sculpture. Works on Paper*, Hatje Cantz, Ostfildern-Ruit 1999, p.70

16. Both Franz Meyer and Ann Gibson have explored this connection, not particularly convincingly. See Franz Meyer, 'Giacometti et Newman' in *Alberto Giacometti sculptures, peintures, dessins*, exhibition catalogue, Musée d'Art Moderne de la Ville de Paris, Paris 1991, pp.59–65 and Ann Gibson, 'Barnett Newman and Alberto Giacometti', *Issue*, spring/summer 1985, pp.2–9

17. Interview with Barnett Newman in David Sylvester, *Interviews with American Artists*, Chatto and Windus, London 2001, p.37. This is a re-edited version of 'Interview with David Sylvester' as presented in *Selected Writings*. There are minor differences between these texts but they have no bearing on the arguments I present. The later version is quoted.

18. 'The reason that I say this, when I painted this painting, which I call Onement, my first Onement, so to speak, I stayed with that painting about eight, nine months, wondering to myself what I had done. What was it?' 'Interview with Emilio de Antonio' in *Selected Writings*, p.306

19. Sylvester interview, p.39. The version in *Selected Writings* is slightly different, p.256

20. G.W.F. Hegel, *The Phenomenology of Spirit*, translated by A.V. Miller, Oxford, New York, Toronto and Melbourne 1977, p.111

21. 'The Mirror Stage as Formative Function of the I as Revealed in Psychoanalytic Experience', reprinted in *Jacques Lacan Écrits, a Selection*, translated by Alan Sheridan, London 1977, pp.1–7

22. Ibid., p.1

23. Ibid., p.2. The italics are Lacan's.

24. Bice Benvenuto and Roger Kennedy, *The Works of Jacques Lacan, an Introduction*, London 1986, p.57

25. Malcolm Pines, 'Mirroring and Child Development: Psychodynamic and Psychological Interpretations' in *Circular Reflections. Selected Papers on Group Analysis and Psychoanalysis*, London and Philadelphia 1998, p.49

26. Newman denied that he preconceived his paintings. 'The fact is, I am an intuitive painter, a direct painter. I have never worked from sketches, never planned a painting, never "thought out" a painting'. '"Frontiers of Space" Interview with Dorothy Gees Seckler' in *Selected Writings*, p.248. There are, however, a number of small sketches in the Newman archive that indicate that he did try out ideas informally. Moreover, a number of drawings closely resemble paintings, even if they are not exact studies for them. Finally, the application of masking tape to a painting is an equivalent to drawing in that it is removable and replaceable.

27. *Selected Writings*, p.36

28. 'Reflections on Mirroring' in Malcolm Pines, op. cit., p.24. Pines acknowledges here the work of a number of other writers on the subject.

29. See Alexandre Kojève, *Introduction to the Reading of Hegel*, edited by Allan Bloom, translated by James H. Nichols, Jr, New York and London 1969, pp. 7–9

30. *Selected Writings*, p.189

31. 'Exhibition of the United States of America' in *Selected Writings*, p.187

32. Lawrence Alloway, 'The Stations of the Cross and the Subjects of the Artist' in *Barnett Newman: The Stations of the Cross, Lema Sabachthani,* exhibition catalogue, Solomon R. Guggenheim Museum, New York 1966, p.11

33. Christopher Macann, *Four Phenomenological Philosophers,* London 1993, p.144

34. 'The Painting of Tamayo and Gottlieb' in *Selected Writings,* p.76

35. In *The Birth of Tragedy,* with which Newman was familiar, Nietzsche contended that one of the doctrines of tragedy is that 'individuation is the primal source of all evil'. Friedrich Nietzsche, 'The Birth of Tragedy' in Raymond Geuss and Ronald Speirs (eds.), *The Birth of Tragedy and Other Writings,* Cambridge 1999, p.52

36. For a discussion of the concept of the 'lost object' as the mother and of matricide as a necessary part of the process of individuation, see Julia Kristeva, *Black Sun,* translated by Leon S. Roudiez, Columbia University Press, New York 1989, p.28

37. Dermot Moran, *Introduction to Phenomenology,* London 2000, p.240

38. Sigmund Freud, 'Beyond the Pleasure Principle' in *On Metapsychology: The Theory of Psychoanalysis,* The Penguin Freud Library, vol.11, translated by James Strachey, compiled and edited by Angela Richards, London 1984, p.310

39. Ibid., p.308

40. See Friedrich Nietzsche, op. cit., pp.52–3 where Nietzsche claims that Dionysiac art breaks 'the spell of individuation'.

41. 'Pre-Columbian Stone Sculpture' in *Selected Writings,* p.64

42. 'Painting and Prose/Frankenstein', ibid., p.89

43. 'The First Man was an Artist', ibid., p.160

44. Ibid., p.159

45. Sigmund Freud, op. cit., p.315. The italics are Freud's.

46. Quoted in J. Laplanche and J-B. Pontalis, *The Language of Psychoanalysis,* translated by Donald Nicholson-Smith, London 1973, 1988 edition, p.112

47. '"Frontiers of Space" interview with Dorothy Gees Seckler' in *Selected Writings,* p.287. Newman repeatedly revised his essays and even his letters, often writing numerous drafts of the same text until he was satisfied with it. The compulsion to re-work, to re-visit and to revise was a strongly marked characteristic. 'The Plasmic Image' is a prime example of this.

48. Friedrich Nietzsche, op. cit., p.40

49. 'Surrealism and the War' in *Selected Writings,* p.95. In 1967 he stated that the War left artists feeling in a 'moral crisis ... it was impossible to paint the kind of paintings that we were doing – flowers, reclining nudes, and people playing the cello'. 'Response to the Reverend Thomas F. Matthews' in *Selected Writings,* p.287

50. 'A New Sense of Fate' in *Selected Writings,* p.169

51. Thomas B. Hess, *Barnett Newman,* exhibition catalogue, Tate Gallery, London 1972, p.32

52. See the chapter titled 'Working with Women Survivors of the Holocaust' in Dinora Pines, *A Woman's Unconscious Use of her Body,* London 1993.

53. T.W. Adorno, 'Commitment' in Arato and Gebhardt (eds.), *The Essential Frankfurt School Reader,* New York 1975, p.312

54. 'Pre-Columbian Stone Sculpture' in *Selected Writings,* p.64

55. See note 36.

56. Newman in an interview with Karlis Osis, 1963, quoted in Richard Shiff, 'Whiteout: The Not-Influence Newman Effect' in Ann Temkin (ed.), *Barnett Newman,* exhibition catalogue, Philadelphia Museum of Art, Philadelphia 2002, p.81.

57. J. Laplanche and J.-B. Pontalis, op.cit., p.465

58. 'The First Man Was an Artist' in *Selected Writings,* p.158

59. Julia Kristeva, op.cit., p.43

60. Ibid., p.42

61. Ibid., p.138

62. The repetition of the motif is another echo of the infant who repeatedly looks at himself in the mirror to establish his identity.

63. *Lema Sabachthani,* or *lama sabachthani* as it is sometimes written, was said by Christ on the Cross, according to the Gospel of St Mark, chapter 15, verse 34. It is also the opening verse of Psalm 22. It has therefore both Christian and Jewish resonances.

64. Lawrence Alloway, op. cit., p.11

65. Ibid., pp.13–14. In his statement for *ARTnews* in May 1966 Newman writes of the *Stations:* 'Each painting is total and complete by itself, yet only the fourteen together make clear the wholeness of the single event.' 'The Fourteen Stations of the Cross, 1958–1966' in *Selected Writings,* p.190

66. Sigmund Freud, 'The Uncanny' in *Art and Literature,* The Penguin Freud Library, vol.14, op. cit., pp.356–7.

67. Edmund Burke, *A Philosophical Enquiry into the Origin of Our Ideas of the Sublime and Beautiful,* 1757, second edition 1759, facsimile edition, Menston 1970, p.119

68. Barbara Reise, 'The Stance of Barnett Newman', *Studio International,* vol.179, no.919, February 1970, p.58

69. For the relationship of the frozen moment, or the film still, to painting, see Margaret Iversen, 'In the Blind Field: Hopper and the Uncanny', *Art History,* vol.21, no.3, September 1998, pp.409–29.

70. Thomas Hess, 'Reviews and Previews', *Art News*, December 1962, p.12

71. For an extended discussion of the impact of psychoanalysis on American art of the mid-century see Michael Leja, *Reframing Abstract Expressionism: Subjectivity and Painting in the 1940s*, New Haven and London 1993.

72. Carl Jung, 'The Spiritual Problem of Modern Man' in *Modern Man in Search of a Soul*, translated by Cary F. Baynes, 1933, reprinted London 2000, pp.200–01.

73. Carl Jung, op. cit., p.209

74. 'The First Man was an Artist' in *Selected Writings*, p.158. In 'Art of the South Seas', written in 1946, Newman makes reference to 'modern man' although it is perfectly plausible that he was using this phrase in a conventional sense rather than with the hindsight of Jung. See *Selected Writings*, p.100

75. 'Archaic Man' in Carl Jung, op. cit., p.131

76. E.C. Goossen, 'The Big Canvas', *Art International*, vol.2, no.6, 1958, pp.46 and 47.

77. I am grateful to Phyllis Tuchman for identifying Goossen in this photograph.

78. Allen Kaprow, op. cit., p.55. The italics are Kaprow's.

79. Maurice Merleau-Ponty, *Phenomenology of Perception*, 1962, translated by Colin Smith, London 1962, reprinted 2000, pp.xvi–xvii

80. See Dermot Moran, op. cit., p.126

81. 'Response to the Reverend Thomas F. Matthews' in *Selected Writings*, p.287

82. '"Frontiers of Space" Interview with Dorothy Gees Seckler' in *Selected Writings*, p.248

83. Dermot Moran, op. cit., p.134

84. Husserl quoted in Moran, op. cit., p.168

85. Maurice Merleau-Ponty, op. cit., p.203

86. In a statement pinned to the wall at Betty Parsons Gallery in 1951, Newman urged the visitor to view his works from close up.

87. Jean-Paul Sartre, *Being and Nothingness*, translated by Hazel E. Barnes, London 1958, reprinted 1972, p.9

88. 'Interview with Emile de Antonio' in *Selected Writings*, p.306

89. Allen Kaprow, op. cit., p.55

90. Merleau-Ponty, op. cit., p.68

91. Alex Potts, *The Sculptural Imagination: Figurative, Modernist, Minimalist*, New Haven and London 2000, p.222. In addition to Potts's chapter 'The Phenomenological Turn', see Brendan Prendeville, 'Merleau-Ponty, Realism and Painting: psychological space and the space of exchange', *Art History*, vol.22, September 1999, pp.364–88 for a useful discussion of Merleau-Ponty's theories as applied to art.

92. Harold Rosenberg, *Barnett Newman*, New York 1978, plate 41

93. See illustrations in Ann Temkin (ed.), *Barnett Newman*, exhibition catalogue, Philadelphia Museum of Art, Philadelphia 2002, p.43 and p.46

94. Sylvester, op.cit., p.40. The earlier version in *Selected Writings* (pp.257-8) is very slightly different in that Newman states that he distrusts the episodic.

95. Interview with Lane Slate in *Selected Writings*, p.253

96. Ibid., p.272

97. 'The Case for "Exporting" Nation's Avant-Garde Art', interview with Andrew Hudson in *Selected Writings*, p.272

98. 'Ohio', *Selected Writings*, pp.174–5

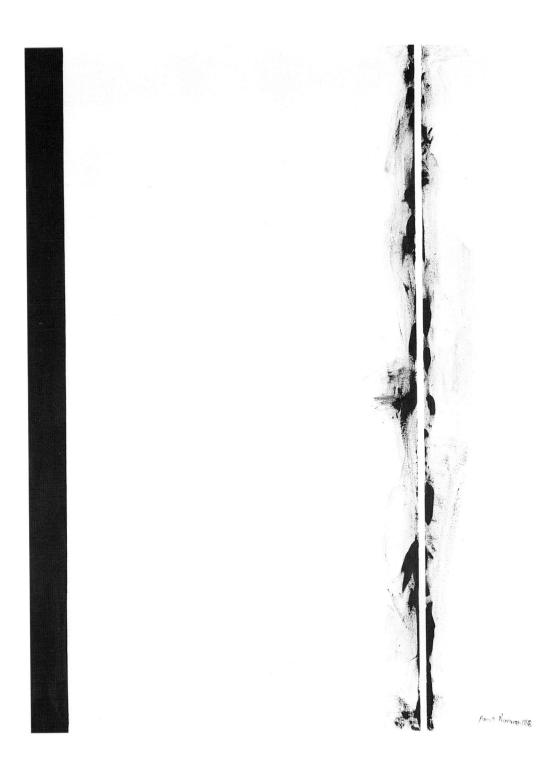

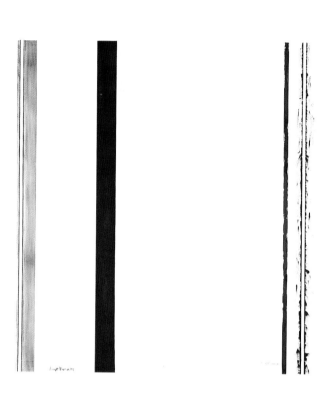

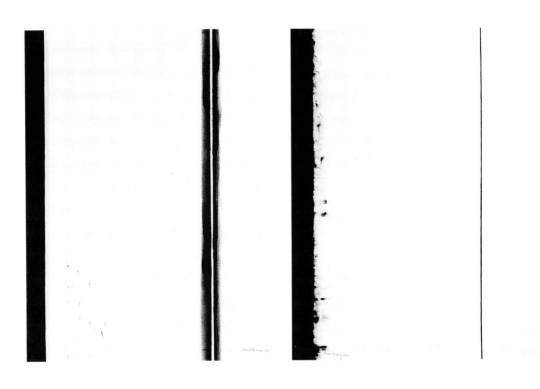

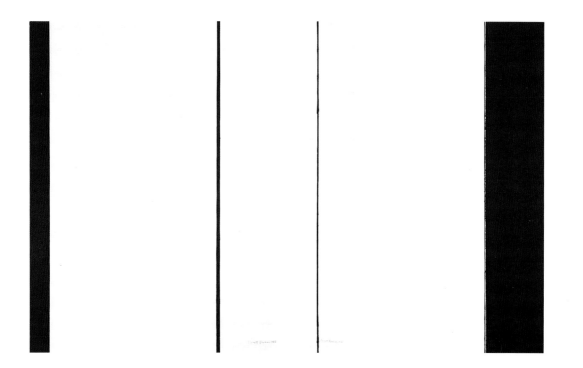

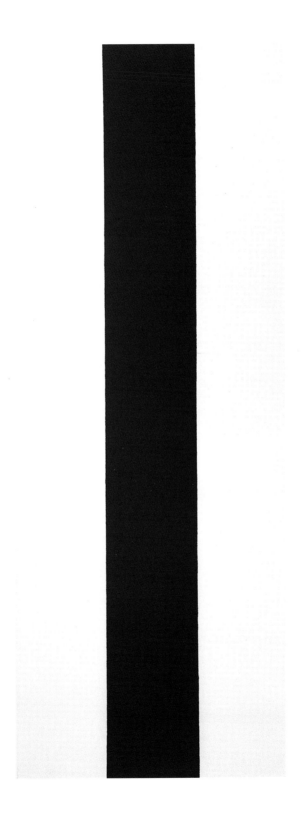

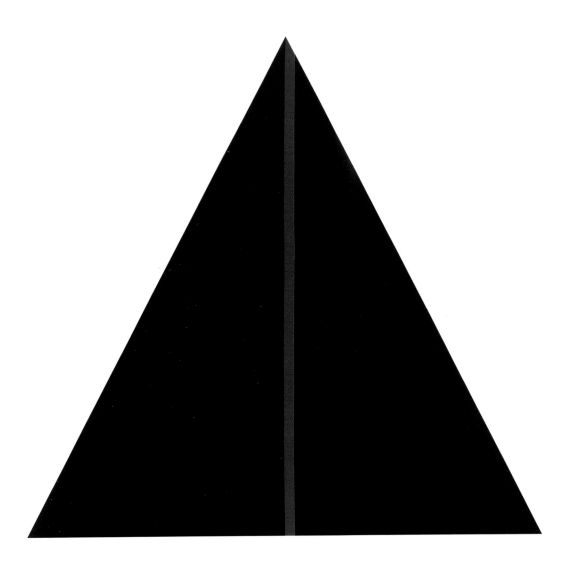

p.45
The Command
1946
Oil on canvas
121.9 x 91.4 cm
Öffentliche
Kunstsammlung
Basel, Kunstmuseum
Basel

p.46
Abraham
1949
Oil on canvas
210.2 x 87.7 cm
The Museum of
Modern Art, New York

p.47
The Promise
1949
Oil on canvas
130.8 x 173 cm
Whitney Museum
of American Art,
New York

p.48
The Wild
1950
Oil on canvas
243 x 4.1 cm
The Museum of
Modern Art, New York

p.49
The Name II
1950
Oil and Magna on
canvas
274.3 x 243.8 cm
National Gallery of
Art, Washington, D.C.

p.50–51
Vir Heroicus Sublimis
1950–51
Oil on canvas
242.2 x 541.7 cm
The Museum of
Modern Art, New York

p.52–53
Cathedra
1951
Oil and Magna on
canvas
243.8 x 541 cm
Stedlijk Museum,
Amsterdam

p.54
Eve
1950
Oil on canvas
238.8 x 172.1 cm
Tate, London

p.55
Adam
1951–52
Oil on canvas
242.9 x 202.9 cm
Tate, London

p.56–57
Uriel
1955
Oil on canvas
243.8 x 548.6 cm
Collection Onnasch

p.58
First Station
1958
Magna on canvas
197.8 x 153.7 cm
p.54–65: National
Gallery of Art,
Washington, D.C.

p.59, left
Second Station
1958
Magna on canvas
198.4 x 153.2 cm
p.59, right
Third Station
1960
Oil on canvas
198.4 x 152.1 cm

p.60, left
Fourth Station
1960
Oil on canvas
198.1 x 153 cm
p.60, right
Fifth Station
1962
Oil on canvas
198.7 x 153 cm

p.61, left
Sixth Station
1962
Oil on canvas
198.4 x 152.1 cm
p.61, right
Seventh Station
1964
Oil on canvas
198.1 x 152.4 cm

p.62, left
Eighth Station
1964
Oil on canvas
198.4 x 152.4 cm
p.62, right:
Ninth Station
1964
Acrylic on canvas
198.1 x 152.7 cm

p.63, left
Tenth Station
1965
Magna on canvas
198.1 x 152.5 cm
p.63, right:
Eleventh Station
1965
Acrylic on canvas
198.1 x 152.4 cm

p.64, left
Twelfth Station
1965
Acrylic on canvas
198.1 x 152.4 cm
p.64, right
Thirteenth Station
1965–66
Acrylic on canvas
198.2 x 152.5 cm

p.65
Fourteenth Station
1965–66
Acrylic and Duco on
canvas
198.1 x 152.2 cm

p.66
The Third
1962
Oil on canvas
257.8 x 305.4 cm
Walker Art Center,
Minneapolis

p.67
The Moment I
1962
Oil on canvas
259.1 x 304.8 cm
Kunsthaus Zürich

p.68
*Who's Afraid of Red,
Yellow and Blue II*
1967
Acrylic on canvas
304.8 x 259.1 cm
Staatsgalerie Stuttgart

p.69
Queen of the Night II
1967
Acrylic on canvas
275.3 x 121.6 cm
Collection of Milly
and Arne Glimcher,
New York

p.70
Now II
1967
Acrylic on canvas
335.9 x 127.3 cm
The Menil Collection,
Houston

p.71
White Fire IV
1968
Acrylic and oil on
canvas
355.2 x 127 cm
Öffentliche
Kunstsammlung
Basel, Kunstmuseum
Basel

p.72–73
Anna's Light
1968
Acrylic on canvas
275 x 610.5 cm
Kawamura Memorial
Museum of Art,
Sakura

p.74
Jericho
1968–69
Acrylic on canvas
269.2 x 285.8 cm
Musée National d'Art
Moderne, Centre
Georges Pompidou,
Paris

p.75
Chartres
1969
Acrylic on canvas
305 x 289.5 cm
Daros Collection,
Switzerland

p.76
Be I (Second Version)
1970
Acrylic on canvas
283.2 x 213.4 cm
The Detroit Institute
of Arts

Newman on Art

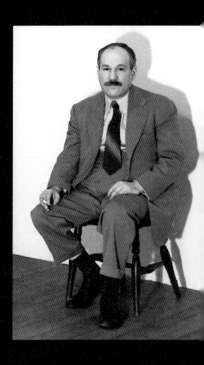

1. Pre-Columbian Stone Sculpture

In 1944 Betty Parsons, who was running a small gallery below the Wakefield bookshop on East 55th street, commissioned Newman to organise an exhibition of pre-Columbian objects. Newman assembled works from a variety of sources including the collections of John Graham, the emigré Russian painter who had known Picasso in Paris and had a keen interest in Jung, Frank Crowninshield, a collector of tribal art whom Graham advised, and the American Museum of Natural History. Newman wrote a short introduction to the exhibition brochure but was later commissioned by Luis J. Navascués, editor of *La Revista Belga*, to write an article on the subject for his magazine. Based in New York, the magazine was a Belgian government organ for wartime propaganda targeted at a South American audience. Newman's article was translated into Spanish and published in August 1944 as 'Escultura precolombina en piedra'.[1]

The wartime context accounts for Newman's introduction of the theme of common links and friendship between North and South America and post-war unity. Newman argues that geographical and political divisions can be healed through a shared culture and an appreciation of art. He identifies pre-Columbian art as a common cultural inheritance of North and South America. Furthermore, he declares that the works on display manifest concerns relevant to today's society and highlights the theme of death. Newman announces here his own interest in an art that emanated from 'the depth of the soul' in which the artist sought salvation. There was a commonality between the art of the present and the art of the past such that the word 'primitive' had no meaning. Finally, in drawing attention to the purity of the exhibition – only sculptures were shown in the gallery space while jewellery and small figurines were shown in the bookshop – Newman indicates a preference for a pared-down aesthetic. *JL*

1. Barnett Newman, 'Escultura pre-Columbina
enpiedra', *La Revista Belga*, vol.1, no.6, August 1944,
pp.51–9

A friendship between peoples that is founded only on a common danger must be ephemeral. When the war is over, when that danger is overcome, will it mean a dividing of the road for North and South America? Shall we then look for a new friendship based on business?

If friendship between the Americas is to be permanent, we must build on a moral principle. All of us know that friendship based on utility is accidental and impermanent. Permanent friendship resembles, as Aristotle explains, a moral state. It can be achieved only if we strive toward an understanding of the moral base of our peoples. In art, the tangible expression of man's innermost, intangible, spiritual aspirations, we have a great school for interhuman learning. Through art, we comprehend the deep stirrings of man's soul. Friendship based on the comprehension of each other's art will be founded, therefore, on a common moral purpose and will do a great deal to accomplish the world unity we all desire, since it is by comprehending the spiritual aspirations of human beings that permanent bonds can best be built.

It is a hopeful sign for our cultural rapprochement to watch the growing aesthetic appreciation of pre-Columbian art. For here we have ready-made, so to speak, a large body of art which should unite all the Americas since it is the common heritage of both hemispheres. An inter-American understanding of our common cultural inheritance should act as a catalytic agent to draw together the inheritors. Here in this art is the moral base for that intercultural community that is the foundation of permanent friendship.

It was therefore fitting at this time that I was invited by Mrs. B. B. Parsons of the Wakefield Gallery, New York, to organize and assemble an exhibition of pre-Columbian stone sculpture. With the help of the American Museum of Natural History and many collectors, we brought together outstanding examples of the art of the Valley of Mexico, of Costa Rica, Guatemala, and Brazil, produced before the white man destroyed their cultures.

It was our particular purpose to bring to the attention of the New York public the artistic expression of the American past that was less familiar from the point of view of both style and medium. We therefore presented the art of the archaic horizon through the work of the Guerrero [Mexico], early Costa Rica, and Brazil regions; the art of the middle horizon through the work of the Totonac, Toltec, Huastec, and Chorotega cultures; the Aztec horizon through early and later works of that period. (We excluded the Maya culture because it is so much better known.) We deliberately limited the exhibition to stone sculpture so that the visitor would get a clear view of the span of this art within a single medium.

It was an exciting experience to see this sculpture presented purely from an aesthetic point of view, freed from the distractions of the usual ethnological jumble of sculpture, pottery, textiles, and other artifacts, which, although of genuine interest to the student of archaeology and ethnology, is a source of confusion to those looking for an aesthetic experience. Here the sculpture was to be enjoyed – as sculpture.

What is there in this sculpture that means so much to the modern mind? We have come to realize that these sculptors were interested in the elemental mystery of life, not in the flippant facts of the transitory life around them. We today are still concerned with the same problem. When the pre-Columbian sculptor handled stone, he sought to capture the meaning of life. Not only in his idols and sacred figures but even in his carved vessels and metates for corn grinding, he depicted his deities. These vessels were always in the form of jaguars or serpents, those strange embodiments of a supervitality, or monkeys, those mysterious creatures that look like men yet are not.

In the little figures of the Guerrero culture that we know with certainty were carved without benefit of metal tools during the archaic period, we already see that abstract quality of formal relationships which tells us more of man's nature than a naturalistic representation of man's physical contours.

In the art of Costa Rica, we find the same desire to catch the secret of nature's power. The head of a jaguar, which was probably the ornamental head of a tremendous ceremonial metate, so characteristic of that region, shows how the artist has caught the brutality of life, the ferocity of nature. No less intense is the Totonac "yoke" with its restrained expression of animal power. At the same time, the artist could rise to heights of grandeur, as in the Huastec goddesses with their Egyptian-like expression of lofty dignity.

Even in the smaller pieces, in the masks, as in the Toltec example, there is that same elemental expression. In these masks is the best expression yet made by an artist of the greatest of all life's mysteries – death. It can be said that theirs was a religious art cut out of the depth of man's soul. The Aztec sacred figure has a pathos unsurpassed by the religious art of Western Europe.

The New York art public found that these arts held for them a personal message. They were no longer the historical curiosities of a forgotten people, the crude expression of a primitive, undeveloped people. Rather, they were the sublime creation of highly sophisticated artists with the same doubts, the same wonderings, and the same searching for salvation, that same indomitable courage which activates men of spirit today. Here indeed was the expression and preoccupation with the problems of our own spirit.

This realization is not an easy one for Americans in an Anglo-Saxon country. In the South American and Central American countries where the aboriginal Indians were able to maintain themselves, and where they and their cultures have become part and parcel of the superimposed European cultures, it is an easier process to understand each other. In the United States, where the Indian has been almost completely destroyed, where the influence of Indian cultures is minor, and in the arts nonexistent, an understanding of ancient American art is more difficult. That the American public responded with so much enthusiasm is a source of great satisfaction and a good omen for the future.

We here are beginning to realize that we should abandon our condescending attitude toward the "primitive" label with all of its confusing implications of childlike perceptions. Can we rightfully assume that these works are the product of an artless, child like mind? Are these the best "primitive" man could do? We are beginning to understand that those masterpieces are the best any man can do.

Paradoxically enough, while we transcend time and place to participate in the spiritual life of a forgotten people, their art by the same magic illuminates the work of our time, of our own sculptors. The sense of dignity, the high seriousness of purpose, the sublime plane of "moral state" evident in this sculpture makes clearer to us why our modern sculptors were compelled to discard the mock heroic, the voluptuous, the superficial realism, the exercise of virtuosity that inhabited the medium for so many European centuries.

* * *

2. The Problem of Subject Matter

In 1944 Newman translated the writings on Impressionism by Jules Laforgue, the nineteenth-century French poet and critic. It must have been around this time that he wrote this article, which remained unpublished in his lifetime. Here Newman asserts that the origins of modern art lay in Impressionism, which liberated colour from the tyranny and excessive decoration of the Venetian school. He castigates the English art critics, Clive Bell and Herbert Read, at that time probably the most widely read critics in the world, for arguing that modern art was simply a seamless continuation of a centuries-old tradition of painting, rather than recognising it as a radical break from that. Where Impressionism emphasised light, Post-Impressionist artists, Newman argues, reintroduced an emphasis on form and, with that, subject matter. The way was open, therefore, for the contemporary artist to employ these radical, technical breakthroughs to make art that had truly contemporary relevance. *JL*

If we could describe the art of this, the first half of the twentieth century, in a phrase, it would read as "the search for something to paint"; just as were we to do the same for modern art as a whole, it must read as "the critical preoccupation of artists with solving the *technical* problems of the painting medium."

Here is the dividing line in the history of art! Whereas every serious artist throughout history has had to solve the problems of his medium, it had always been personal, a problem of talent. It was not until the impressionists that a group of artists set themselves a communal task: the exploration of a technical problem together. With them, talent became axiomatic. What to do with it? That [question] has become the earmark of modern art movements. This critical reevaluation of the artist's role, this refusal to continue blindly the ritual of what art professors like to call tradition, has become a dividing line in art that is sharp indeed. For were all knowledge, written and oral, of the dates of production of those great works that make up the art treasury of Western Europe to be lost (let us hope the work is not), [the body of work] from Veronese to Delacroix would become a dateless jumble. No man could trace its chronological progress with accuracy, so unified is its general appearance. Were this jumble, however, to include the work of anybody after Courbet, beginning with the impressionists, it would segregate itself at once. For good or bad, impressionism has given art an unmistakably different look.

This heretical insistence on a dividing line may provoke those critics, from Clive Bell to Herbert Read, who have made careers for themselves as "friends of modern art" by broadcasting the sophism that the values of modern art were a continuation of the great tradition of European painting begun in the Renaissance. Impelled, perhaps, by the Englishman's innate aversion to revolution, these critics devoted themselves to talking everybody out of its revolutionary character. The shrewd popularization of the big lie that modern art isn't modern succeeded in establishing the position of respectability modern art now enjoys with museum directors and professional art lovers, but it wreaked havoc with the creative forces struggling for a footing, wherever this false thesis took root. It goes a long way toward explaining the intellectual barrenness and sterility that dominates the art of the English-reading world, for it is the critic who sets the tone of the audiences of art.

It can now be seen that the art critics who maligned Cézanne during his lifetime had a better understanding of the revolutionary implications of his art than his English and American defenders, who hailed him as the father of modern art on the grounds that he was the great proponent of the art of Poussin. It was the good fortune of the Ecole de Paris that it did not have the protection of such friends. [That] may also explain its fertility, because in Paris the man of talent was able to approach the revolution in art uncorrupted. For it was in its revolutionary differences, in its radicalism, in its "modernism," that this art was able to lay down the basis for a continued creativeness – not in the elaborate and erudite "affinities" with "tradition" that have been read into modern art by its apologists.

Modern painting begins with the impressionists precisely because for the first time in history, a group of artists repudiated the role of the great personal message with its attendant doctrine of the immaculate conception and decided to devote themselves exclusively to solving a technical problem in painting – color. Painting throughout Europe, despite its rugged individualism, had become blanketed by the velvet standards of the school of Venice. Only when the cutting of this velvet surface, begun by Constable and Courbet, culminated in a transfusion of the scientific discoveries of the time concerning the nature of the spectrum into the bloodstream of the painting art; only when Pissarro, Monet, Seurat, et al. created a new color aesthetic was this Venetian velvet finally repudiated to open up a richer world of possibilities. No matter what we may think today of the impressionists as artists, they solved the problem of color for all those painting since. They set the artist's palette free of its prison.

The discovery of a new idea is intoxicating. It was natural that the impressionists, reveling in its exhilaration, should minimize, even disregard, all other art elements. It could not occur to them that drawing and subject matter were problems. The color of light was the problem. The result was inevitably a school of landscape painting, for light, despite our lamps, still means the great outdoors. In that great theater of color, form and shape lose outline. Since the problem of lines does not exist in nature, drawing becomes irrelevant. There also the problem of subject matter finds automatic solution. What to paint? Paint what you see – anything. This automatic subject matter was to produce a laissez-faire eclecticism. Eclecticism is chaos.

The postimpressionists, although not formally or consciously organized, were nevertheless a group in the unity of their opposition to the monist aesthetic of the impressionists. Cézanne, van Gogh, Renoir, like isolated scientists who discover the same truth, formed a community when they reasserted that color, no matter how important its liberation, was still only one of the artist's problems. They realized the necessity of devoting themselves to the exploration of these other elements. Continuing the new role of the artist begun by the impressionists, they reaffirmed, each in his way, that only by understanding the purpose of painting rather than its mechanics, no matter how advanced scientifically, could they arrive at its true nature. Where the impressionists shouted that vision is light, these men made the point that light makes us see – shapes. The result was a reexamination of the mechanics of drawing and form.

Cézanne was the first artist to comprehend that in nature there are no lines. Herein lies the significance of his remark that nature is a collection of cubes, cones, and spheres. He saw the world as it is, mass instead of contours. Line could not count: not one exists in nature. It was what was between the lines that mattered. The artist's function is to use, not to draw, what is between the lines. The secret lay in the discovery and use of distortion as a principle. Fundamentally this is Cézanne's great discovery, for where the impressionists used science to discover the hidden resources of the palette, the postimpressionists found that they had to deny scientific perspective.

They were well aware that the impressionists in freeing the palette had only succeeded in enslaving the artist to nature. The real problem, these men felt, was to free art from nature. The postimpressionists solved it by the discovery and use of distortion. The fact is that this principle is better science. It was their skeptical approach to the nature of shapes (which they asserted were lines) that resembles the skepticism of the impressionists, who questioned the makeup of pigment, and is the basis of their critique, which made possible the emancipation of the artist from nature.

It was inevitable that in the concentrating on mass the problem of subject matter should become automatic. For it is in the simplest of shapes that we find the secret of all shapes. Postimpressionism, therefore, was to be a school of still-life painters for men with a Nature Morte critique toward all things.

* * *

3. Painting and Prose/Frankenstein

Newman read widely and frequently wrote responses to articles he appreciated or disagreed with. Here, in an unpublished response to a three-part article by Joseph Frank in the *Sewanee Review*,[1] titled 'Spatial Forms in Modern Literature', Newman began to formulate a manifesto for what would become his mature idiom as a painter. After setting out his agreement with Frank, namely that modern painting and literature share an interest in space, he states that Frank failed to recognise that space had always been a literary theme. Whereas the writers of the nineteenth century were preoccupied with mimesis and created the illusion of three-dimensionality, twentieth-century writers and painters destroyed the third dimension, forcing the viewer and reader to remain detached and outside the painting or narrative. Painting, Newman argues, has developed a new language, or rather a language which itself has become a focus of attention. However, for Newman this is insufficient to constitute high art. Art should be a 'vehicle for human expression' and should take its cue from pre-Christian culture which was concerned with the numinous expressed in epic form. Newman indicates here an ambition to work on a large scale but to do so the artist must communicate a large moral theme of universal significance. To find that theme was the problem for the contemporary painter. In essence, Newman's interest was no different from that of late eighteenth-century French artists who, tired of the frippery of Rococo art, created a new art that employed Greek and Roman myths to promote contemporary values and comment on contemporary events. Newman's response to Frank, which Frank never saw, was drafted a number of times. 'Painting and Prose' is the most complete draft. *JL*

1. Joseph Frank, 'Spatial Forms in Modern Literature', *Sewanee Review*, vol.53, pp.221–40, 433–56 and 643–53

Joseph Frank, in a recent article in the *Sewanee Review*, explains modern literature by introducing a comparison with modern painting and makes the point that T. S. Eliot, Proust, and Joyce handled the literary form not as a continuity in time, progressing from one point to another logically, but as a problem in space, organizing fragments so that they unite in space to produce the aesthetic effect. This is perhaps one of the most valuable analyses of modern literature to appear in recent times; but there is another point of comparison between literature and painting which Mr. Frank has failed to touch upon, which is as important for a proper understanding of modern literature as a possible key to its future development: that the modern prose writer has followed the modern painter in his attitude to artistic language. In other words, the modern prose writer uses words in the same way that the modern painter uses line and color; and just as the modern painter has forsaken the use of line and color to present a visual object in order to have these elements speak for and in themselves, so the modern writer has given up using the language to project objects in a reality, and instead allows words and sentences to speak and to produce the aesthetic effect within themselves. This revolution, understandable in painting, has been overlooked in literature.

Where Mr. Frank's argument breaks down is on the fact that literature has always been spatial. The spatial concept in literature is not necessarily recent, the discovery of Proust and Joyce. Dickens, Thackeray, Tolstoy utilized a spatial concept in their work. The question is not therefore as he sees it, that one did and the other did not use space; the question that should be studied is, What kind of space did the modern writer use?

Tolstoy followed the space concept prevalent in the painting of his time, which was three-dimensional. He and the novelists of that time used words in such a way that the reader looked through them as through a window into the field or landscape in which the action and life of the novel took place – just as in the painting of that time color was similarly used to bring the onlooker into the picture, to look through the picture as through a window into a deep box or landscape, to participate with the figures and objects of the picture. The modern painter, however, introduced a new concept of space into painting where the third dimension was destroyed, preventing us from entering the picture and thus keeping us outside, compelling us to contemplate the painter's language and thereby forcing us to react to the painter's use of the language. The modern writer has borrowed this new spatial concept. No longer do we need, or is it expected of us, to transcend the verbal veil to get into the book. The modern novelist compels us to react to the words themselves by destroying the three-dimensional idea and by presenting his concept through whatever action or characters he creates, flat on the page. Thus we see that Mr. Frank comes close to the problem of modern literature but actually misses the point, for only a thorough understanding of the modern concept of space can help us explain modern literature.

Surrealism in art was a return to deep space, where through the traditional window of realistic painting, the surrealist was able to make us enter his world of fancy. He was able to intensify and make us believe in his world of imagination by his use of an overdeveloped, heightened realism. This had its reflection in writing when the surrealist prose writers used a "heightened" realism in the choice of words to make real the paradox of their imagery and metaphor.

There has been a lot of to-do about [*Les chants de*] *Maldolor* [by Lautréamont], to whom the surrealists look as father of their movement. He is so only insofar as he developed their imaginary subject matter. It is true that he helped the surrealists find their subject matter. But the surrealists got their "language" and their techniques from the great writer Joyce. It was Joyce who taught the surrealists how to use words as if they were clay that could be molded and shaped to produce a plastic form. They have never paid their debt to Joyce. Were it not for him surrealism could never have arisen, and *Finnegans Wake* is the most intense and compact surrealist work yet produced.

It may seem from these paragraphs that I fall into the prevalent attitude of modern criticism that sees recent literary movements as resulting from similar movements in painting, whereas the fact is exactly the other way. The driving force of modern painting has been to change, to reconstitute the painting medium from a photographic technique of realistic rendering (after the rise of photography made [the nature of painting] clear) into a medium capable of pure expression. Modern painting is an attempt to change painting into a poetic language, to make pigment expressive rather than representational.

It is in poetry that the problem of handling a realistic tool, a tool that permits of realism without being realistic, has been best solved. In music, the pure abstract element of tone has made it easy. Sometimes attempts have been made in music to imitate naturalistic sounds, but those attempts are unnatural and not very usual. It is easier and more natural for music to deliver its message, to present its concepts, in terms of the abstract nature of notes of sound. In music there is never an attempt to relate sound to any conventional prejudice, or natural sound, whereas in literature and in painting it is natural for us to associate the word or the painted object with the thing *in* nature, to combine its evocative nature with its appearance. In poetry, however, the element of music contained in it has permitted the artist to approach that abstract handling of the language usual in music, so that we have learned to react to poetry in a purely abstract way, or, in other words, to react to the words themselves. The whole drive of poetry, therefore, and in recent times of painting and prose, has been in the direction of music, to divorce the languages of literature and of painting from the confusing dichotomy of meaning inherent in their media so that they would function purely and abstractly in the manner of musical notes.

Modern painting is characterized also by a reexamination of its aesthetic base, by comparison with the art of other traditions and times, and also by a concern with – or more correctly, a return to – its primitive function, that is, its original function as a vehicle of human expression. The modern painter has therefore studied carefully the art of primitive peoples all over the world and particularly the art of archaic Western Europe in an attempt to discover the original impulse. In painting we have learned that the primitive artist was never concerned with the scene around him or with the expression of human problems arising from human relationships. Neither was he concerned with the expression of individual human feelings. Ancient art was preoccupied with the creation of gods, with the expression of forces, with numinous beings. We realize that with the rise of Christianity this activity was removed from man by a rationalized religion and also that with the rise of Judaism, this activity was removed from man by an outright taboo. The renaissance in modern painting can be attributed to the deliberate attempt on the part of artists to return to the artist's prime function.

A similar attempt, certainly a similar study on the part of writers might be equally fruitful. Surely that would be a better type of imitation than the attempt to transfer into literature the actual discoveries made by painters in their own medium that may not necessarily fit into the medium of writing.

It is extremely difficult to do this in literature because the art of writing came so much later than the art of sculpting, for example, so that a good deal of literature, which in its primitive form must have been oral, has been lost. A good deal of early writing, like the Etruscan and Cretan, has never been translated. Enough remains, and enough is known, however, to make clear that the primitive writer and the archaic writer were, like the artists of their time, never concerned with the history of the tribe or the mundane problems of human relationships that have become the stock-in-trade of Western Europe: love, the triangle, the social problem, themselves.

Most early writing of all traditions and of all peoples has been in the form of the epic, and its subject matter has usually been numinous – a concern with how the gods lived, what the gods did, etc. Homer combined this preoccupation with divine matters together with the historic events of his country, so that although he worked in the epic form, he reduced it to a human – or, rather, a social – level, depicting the interplay of gods and men.

Some of the modern writers have attempted a modern epic. They have usually been the best writers of our time. Joyce did this with *Ulysses*, setting out to create an epic prose poem of Dublin. The fact that he called it *Ulysses* is an index to his motives. Proust likewise created an epic. It is not, however, enough for a modern writer to return to the epic. That can be his technical approach, but he must also discover the proper subject matter to make such an epic possible at the present time. It is not enough to use a large canvas and make a literary work encompass a wide and large theme, which is what most critics believe to be the definition of an epic. The subject matter of epics, it is true, is a large theme, but it must be a large *moral* theme if the writer is at all to catch any part of the absolute. Such a theme, projected in the abstract symbolism of poetry and the poetic style and removed from the confusion of naturalistic representationalism, can become the vehicle for a new literary renaissance, recreating a symbolism that will have elements of fulfillment for all mankind. Most of the true epics of the past have been confined to a local divinity or to a local numinal problem, but the international character of the modern mind, which encompasses diverse traditions, needs a more universal theme to express universal truth than was needed heretofore.

It must be pointed out that the problem is not simply to destroy all appearance, for we have learned in painting that doing so may only create a stylized type of abstraction. Joyce in his *Finnegans Wake* tried to solve the problem of appearance by denying it and succeeded in creating a nonobjective art that has all the disadvantages of nonobjective painting. Just as in nonobjective painting the use of pure shapes creates a stylized design surface devoid of emotional content, so Joyce's use of the pure word-sound creates a puristic art that leaves us cold. One does not solve a problem of subject matter or succeed in separating subject matter from appearance by completely denying subject matter.

The abstract art of the Northwest Coast Indian and the archaic Greek, like the archaic epic, used subject matter. The fact that they were able to transcend appearance and make contact with absolutes was based on the particular *kind* of subject matter they used rather than on the complete avoidance of apparential [sic] subject matter. That is a truth which has become very evident to the new painters who, although dissatisfied with realistic subject matter, are equally dissatisfied with the abstract and nonobjective art of the last thirty years. These painters feel that Picasso, Arp, Kandinsky, and Mondrian have made revealing statements, but that essentially they are negative statements. None of them discovered a new subject matter or recreated an old one; these men took the easy way out and destroyed subject matter. The discoveries of Joyce, particularly of *Finnegans Wake*, are of the same nature. Joyce, Eliot, Pound have escaped the trite subject matter of our Western European literary traditions, but they have done it either by denying it completely or by substituting a religious theme, which by the very nature of its legend is a blind alley. What has to be done is to discover the proper theme that will make contact with reality; what has to be discovered is a new subject matter.

* * *

4. Surrealism and the War

In March 1945, André Breton, the leader of the Surrealist movement and a refugee in New York, wrote an introduction to the catalogue of Arshile Gorky's exhibition at the Julien Levy Gallery in which he harnessed Gorky to the Surrealist movement.[1] Newman felt that Breton thus threatened to obliterate the American identity of the artists of the 'new direction' in American art by subsuming them within this essentially European movement. Ironically, of course, Gorky was a European artist by origin but it did not suit Newman's propagandistic purpose to admit this. Newman was perhaps the most articulate of the new generation of artists who, while acknowledging their debt to Surrealism, nevertheless asserted their radical independence from it. Surrealism had been shown in New York for more than a decade and was now commonly known. Newman here determines that it is so well known and that the new American painting is so strongly launched that Surrealism has become a historical movement ripe for objective assessment. What Newman valued was the fact that Surrealism was an art of ideas, which expressed contemporary pathos and, in the face of modern art's emphasis on design (here he was thinking of Mondrian and his followers), resurrected the importance of subject matter. Writing at a time when photographs of Nazi concentration camps were reaching Allied nations, Newman declares that Surrealism had been prophetic of the atrocities; that far from being situated in the realm of fantasy, Surrealist painting became a reality. At the same time, Newman takes a swipe at American Marxists whose support of social realism Newman regarded as empty rhetoric. This essay was unpublished in Newman's lifetime. *JL*

1. André Breton, 'The Eye Spring', translated by Julien Levy, *Arshile Gorky*, exhibition catalogue, Julien Levy Gallery, New York 1945

It is natural that surrealism died with the advent of war. For surrealism is dead. Its leaders, Ernst and Tanguy, continue, but their work has now become a continuous performance. The new painters in America have veered off from its influence to follow a new direction.

The best signs of surrealism's decay lie in the attempts Breton has made to find new converts. His pretentious presentations of Donati, who has reduced surrealism to a pretty boudoir painting, exposed how the spring that fed the movement has grown stagnant. The compulsion to fit Gorky into the surrealist formula shows how desperate is its point.

Its real obituary, however, has been the change of attitude of those dealers with whom surrealism found its home. Peggy Guggenheim has converted her gallery so that the surrealists hang in a sort of mausoleum. Julien Levy has assumed the death of surrealism and shows it, whenever he does, as the work of a past era. Both dealers are seeking out the new painters who are no longer painting like the surrealists.

In surrealism's decay it has become the fashion for art critics and artists to kick the dying man. It is perhaps necessary for a new art movement that the men who advance it should rebel against the influence of their forerunners, especially when they constitute an academy. But the new direction is now so happily on its way, the new shoots are now sufficiently strong, that it is possible to evaluate surrealism objectively.

There can be no question that the objections raised to the movement are valid. Its use of old-fashioned perspective, its high realism, its preoccupation with the dream, we now know are not the final answer or the perfect formula for artistic expression. [The surrealist approach] was narrow and had to become sterile.

It is not true, however, that these men were irresponsible, that their subject matter was removed from reality, that their intention was precocious pleasure in the shock of pathological subject matter.

We must not overlook that the great contribution of surrealism was in its revival of subject matter, which had been deliberately avoided by the strong antirealist program of modern art. We can now see much more: that the subject matter of surrealism was the most important of our time and definitely linked to our time.

The surrealists' work was in the nature of prophecy. For the horror they created and the shock they built up were not merely the dreams of crazy men; they were prophetic tableaux of what the world was to see as reality. They showed us the horror of war; and if men had not laughed at the surrealists, if they had understood them, the war might never have been.

No painting exists [that is better surrealism] than the photographs of German atrocities. The heaps of skulls are the reality of Tchelitchew's vision. The mass of bone piles are the reality of Picasso's bone compositions, of his sculpture. The monstrous corpses are Ernst's demons. The broken architecture, the rubble, the grotesque bodies are the surrealist reality. The sadism in those pictures, the horror and the pathos are around us. Had men not laughed at them, they might not have needed to cry at them, to be them, to live in them. Those who saw surrealist works as the esoteric playthings of decadent sophisticates, removed from life, cannot avoid the fact now that these things were the "superreal" mirror of the world to come, of the world of today.

How much closer have these men been to our time than the American Marxists! What is their lesson? That these surrealist Marxists were at least artists, while our American social realists are at best poor journalists.

The attack against the ACA Gallery school of painting has been that these men were political. It is now [proved] a false charge. For the surrealists were political, too; they were Marxists, too. The difference is that whereas the surrealists were politically minded, their realm was the realm of ideas, while the social realists, antiintellectuals swimming in the waters of "life", were only politicians. Here is a fundamental truth: that ideas, even political ideas, can do no harm if the artist is true, if the artist works in the realm of thought. Surrealism taught that ideas can be not only fruitful but important to art. And in reviving subject matter the surrealists showed us a prophecy. In their surrealist world lies the real world, while the world of the social realist is one only of appearances.

The argument against surrealist subject matter was a specious one. [Surrealist subject matter] served its purpose well. But now that World War II is coming to an end it is, for the artist, dated. That is why surrealism as an artistic credo is dead.

All new painting when begun is in the nature of prophecy. That is what the academic dialecticians have now realized. This is what the professional revolutionaries, the left-wing politicians, have never understood, and this is why they are always led into philistinism. What they want is an official art to reflect their official politics. Perhaps this is a clue also to the nature of their revolutionary minds. Concerned with action, they spurn ideas, and their action takes on the form and shape of political academism, whereas the artist interested in ideas maintains a constant revolutionary strain. Here also may be the clue to revolutionary failure. The true revolutionary is so only in idea. Effecting these ideas almost at once makes them obsolete; thus the products of revolution cannot have any relation to the revolutionary concept except to stratify it, and in the end to kill it.

* * *

5. The Plasmic Image

What has become known as 'The Plasmic Image' was written over a period of time in 1945. It was begun sometime after the opening of the Mondrian exhibition at the Museum of Modern Art, New York (21 March – 13 May) and was still in progress after the opening of *A Problem for Critics*, the exhibition organised by the critic, Howard Putzel, at the 67 Gallery (May – June). The article, which is more of a private rumination, took the form of several drafts of which the first and the last parts are printed here. It was never finished.

Here Newman asserts the existence of a new movement in American painting that has its origins in, but deviates from, Surrealism and abstraction, with Gottlieb and Rothko at the forefront. The essay was written before Pollock's breakthrough and shortly after Newman himself began painting. The earliest known works by Newman date from 1945 or possibly late 1944. It has been suggested that Newman destroyed earlier work but it is equally possible that he did not make any earlier paintings but simply talked a good picture.

Newman contends that the new American painters reject the by now academic fantasies of the Surrealists but acknowledges the important contribution the Surrealists made in giving emphasis to subject matter. By contrast the abstract movement shunned subject matter which resulted in another kind of academicism, namely the decorative. The new American painters, Newman writes, adopt an expressionist idiom to paint works with philosophical content: that is, themes linked to myths of universal importance expressive of contemporary history – chaos, creation, life and death. 'Plasmic' is the term he adopts to define this new art, descriptive of its primordial content, the birth of the world. It is also an ironic appropriation and manipulation of the term 'plastic' that Mondrian adopted to describe his own art. *JL*

Part 1

The subject matter of creation is chaos. The present feeling seems to be that the artist is concerned with form, color, and spatial arrangement. This objective approach to art reduces it to a kind of ornament. The whole attitude of abstract painting has been such that it has reduced painting to an ornamental art whereby the picture surface is broken up in geometrical fashion into a new kind of design-image. It is a decorative art built on a slogan of purism where the attempt is made for an unworldly statement.

The failure of abstract painting is due to the confusion that exists in the understanding of primitive art [as well as that] concerning the nature of abstraction. It is now a widespread notion that primitive art is abstract, and that the strength in the primitive statement arises from this tendency toward abstraction. An examination of primitive cultures, however, shows that many traditions were realistic. ... Whatever the tradition, there always existed in the majority of primitive cultures even from prehistoric times a strict division between the geometric abstraction used in the decorative arts and the art of that culture. It is known that strict geometry was the province of the women members of primitive tribes, who used these devices in their weaving, pottery, etc. No case of any primitive culture shows the use of geometric form for religious expression. The men, in most tribes the practicing artists, always employed a symbolic, even a realistic, form of expression.

In primitive tribes distortion was used as a device whereby the artist could create symbols. Clarity will be gained if we define abstraction in the strict terms of the abstract painter, as a field of painting concerned with geometric forms, and if we separate this concept from distortion. One of the serious mistakes made by artists and art critics has been the confusion over the nature of distortion, the easy assumption that any distortion from the realistic form is an abstraction of that form. ...

All artists, whether primitive or sophisticated, have been involved in the handling of chaos. The painter of the new movement clearly understands the separation between abstraction and the art of the abstract. He is therefore not concerned with geometric forms per se but in creating forms that by their abstract nature carry some abstract intellectual content.

There is an attempt being made to assign a surrealist explanation to the use these painters make of abstract forms. The attempt says that inasmuch as these artists are attempting to create a superreality they are therefore offshoots of the surrealist movement. It is not enough, because these painters are working in the realm of imagination, to insist on a linking of two diverse tendencies. Surrealism is interested in a dream world that will penetrate the human psyche. To that extent it is a mundane expression. It is still concerned with the human world; it never becomes transcendental. The present painter is concerned not with his own feelings or with the mystery of his own personality but with the penetration into the world-mystery. His imagination is therefore attempting to dig into metaphysical secrets. To that extent his art is concerned with the sublime. It is a religious art which through symbols will catch the basic truth of life, which is its sense of tragedy.

The present painter can be said to work with chaos not only in the sense that he is handling the chaos of a blank picture plane but also in that he is handling chaos of form. In trying to go beyond the visible and known world he is working with forms that are unknown even to him. He is therefore engaged in a true act of discovery in the creation of new forms and symbols that will have the living quality of creation. No matter what the psychologists say these forms arise from, that they are the inevitable expression of the unconscious, the present painter is not concerned with the process. Herein lies the difference between him and the surrealists. At the same time, in his desire, in his will to set down the ordered truth that is the expression of his attitude toward the mystery of life and death, it can be said that the artist like a true creator is delving into chaos. It is precisely this that makes him an artist, for the Creator in creating the world began with the same material – for the artist tried to wrest truth from the void.

Part 12

Mr. H. Putzel in his recent exhibition [May 14, 1945] at his 67 Gallery, called *A Problem for Critics*, has shown the need of naming and perhaps explaining the new movement in painting that is taking place in America. That such a movement exists – although [it is not organized] in the way the surrealist and cubist movements were organized – is certain. In the art galleries on Fifty-seventh Street, the Whitney Museum Biannual, there has been a spontaneous emergence of what the conservative critics have called a "trend" but which is unmistakably a movement in the direction of "subjective abstraction."

Critics have not been entirely blind to this art movement. James Johnson Sweeney, for example, in his book on Miró, hails him as "not the end product of Picasso but the innovator or father of a new movement," so well typified by these new subjective abstractions. Sidney Janis, in his book *Abstract and Surrealist Art in America*, which is devoted to the two movements that form the basis of the new art, points out – timidly, it is true – the possibility of an "American renaissance" in the combined direction of the work of Rothko, Gottlieb, Gorky, and Motherwell. Clement Greenberg adds Pollock and Baziotes, whom he recognizes as the leaders of this movement. In spite of the overstatement, it indicates that the movement has membership. Even Jewell, who cannot be looked to as a friend of any advance-guard movement, was keen enough to become, as early as 1943, perhaps the first publicly to notice one, for out of the forty-odd artists then showing at the spring annual of the Federation of Modern Painters and Sculptors, he singled out Gottlieb, Rothko, and Schewe as artists embodying a new painting concept in their work. In three Sunday *New York Times* articles he tried to label and belittle this "new" movement as "Globalism." It is significant that Gottlieb and Rothko are now at the forefront of the present trend.

Before we investigate what these painters are doing to entitle them to the classification of an art movement, it is important to understand that only a few of these men, who some believe are combining surrealism and abstract painting, stem from either movement. That is the danger of crystallized movements.

Essentially the new painters were dissatisfied with realism, yet they could not enter into the reactions against realism typified by the abstract and surrealist artists. In the one case they felt it was no solution for the painter dissatisfied with cheap subject matter to deny it entirely – that is like curing a case of chilblains by cutting the leg off. These men considered that the artistic problem was not whether they should or should not have subject matter; the problem was, What kind of subject matter?

At the same time they could not accept the dream world of the surrealists as the proper answer, especially since, with the exception of Miró, the surrealists were reviving ultrasurrealistic, almost academic techniques. Instead of illustrating literary and historical subject matter à la Ernest Meissonier, the surrealists used a similar realism to make vivid the fantasy objects and images of the dream world – a perfect technique for that purpose. Once, however, the shock of this new world is overcome, the esoteric and strange imagery become "normal" and a new but persistent boredom, the boredom of recognition, [sets in]. It was inevitable that the surrealists' world of the imagination should reach a cul-de-sac of invention. In surrealism the forces of fancy acted on by the pressure of realism [result in] fatigue. In New York, it is now admitted that surrealism is dead. [But] while the dying are being kicked, it is well to remember that surrealism has made a contribution to the aesthetic of our time by emphasizing the importance of subject matter for the painter.

Abstract art in America has to a large extent been the preoccupation of the dull, who by ignoring subject matter remove themselves from life to engage in a pastime of decorative art. The best that can be said for this abstract art is that it is elegant, handsome, a very fine kind of modern arabesque. Even the stimulus of Mondrian has done little to change the character of the work, though his example as artist and man has created respect for the steadfastness to principle these artists have maintained.

It is only natural that the artists working outside the rim of the three movements of journalistic realism, Freudian realism, and puristic design should find their place in expressionism. For expressionism gave them the opportunity for personal commentary on the world around them, although a great deal of this commentary revolved around a morbid sensibility and sentimentality. The good American artists in this movement were able to project some deeply felt emotion that approached the profound. It was, however, a risky aesthetic, because the emphasis on feeling had a tendency to shut out intellectual content. If it were possible to define the essence of this new [American] movement, one might say that it was an attempt to achieve feeling through intellectual content. The new pictures are therefore philosophic. In handling philosophic concepts which per se are of an abstract nature, it was inevitable that the painters' form should be abstract. In the sense that these pictures try to say something – that is, that they have a subject – it was equally inevitable that the abstract form should have surrealist overtones.

* * *

6. Art of the South Seas

In early 1946 the Museum of Modern Art, New York, mounted an exhibition of objects from the Oceanic islands of the South Pacific. Newman was commissioned to review it for *Ambos Mundos*, a newly launched Spanish language magazine published by the publisher of *La Revista Belga*.[1] Newman reiterates the commonality he sees between 'primitive' art and contemporary American painting, while at the same time commenting on the links between Surrealism and South Sea art. For Newman, however, those links are superficial, indicating that the surrealists misunderstood the art of earlier cultures. What they had not understood was that for the Oceanic artists art was an expression of reality, whereas Newman interprets Surrealism as an expression of fantasy. He thereby paves the way for his conclusion that the new American painting is the true inheritor of the Oceanic tradition for it is an art without illusion, expressive of universal myths directly experienced. Against the background of the war Newman describes how the 'primitive' artist and the contemporary artist, or 'modern man' as he puts it, thereby invoking the writings of Carl Jung, experienced terror. Their art emerged as a direct response to it, as a search for salvation. This article is also notable for a brief but important reference to Newman's awareness of Sigmund Freud. *JL*

1. Barnett Newman, 'Las formas artisticas del Pacifico', *Ambos Mundos*, vol.1, no.1, June 1946, pp.51–5. Reprinted in English as 'Art of the South Seas', *Studio International*, vol.179, no.919, February 1970, pp.70–1

Primitive art has become for artists the romantic dream of our time. Each art epoch, like each historic age, has its romantic dream of the past, since artists, no less than historians, yearn for the great works of some other time, never for the achievements of their own time. The impressionists, it is well known, had their dream in the Japanese print. They doted over this art of the Orient just as, centuries earlier, the Byzantines, anxious to create a sacred art around the Christ legend, had their romance in the religious grandeur of India and China. Until the impressionists broke the spell, Europe's emotional life had been dominated, for centuries, by that grandiose dream, the Renaissance.[1] The

Renaissance itself found its dream in classical Greece. And for the Greeks, the Egyptian pyramid stood as a standard of absolute beauty, the symbol of all their aesthetic hopes.

In our time Picasso may have dreamed of a half-dozen utopias, but his primary dream – the one that gave him his voice – was Negro sculpture. This does not mean that his art arose from it. But Picasso did try to achieve the artistic ideals he thought he understood to exist in this primitive art tradition. Likewise Matisse found his nostalgic world in the great decorative traditions of primitive Persia. The nonobjectivists from Kandinsky to Mondrian yearned for the purism of primitive design. The expressionists seized the idiom of modern art, rooted as this idiom is in an interpretation of the meaning of primitive art, to express a personal art, from within, just as El Greco used the then existing Venetian dream to express his own personal vision. Modern sculpture likewise has its romance in primitive traditions: Brancusi in the prehistoric and the Negro, Henry Moore in pre-Columbian Mexican sculpture, Lipchitz in a succession of primitive styles.

The Museum of Modern Art in New York has brought this interrelationship between modern art and the art of primitive peoples up to date with its recent exhibition of art objects from the Oceanic Islands of the South Pacific. With this exhibition, it is now clear that even surrealism, which has always given the impression of being on the periphery – if not outside the curve – of the modern plastic revolutionary wave, is no exception to the romanticism of our time, that it had its romance in the art of the South Seas.

This has been the most comprehensive display of this art ever assembled and is perhaps the first aesthetic presentation of this material, making it an event of international importance.[2] It is interesting that except for the pieces brought from Australia to represent the art of its aborigines, the four hundred items collected have all come from American science museums. It has taken a war to make the American people tragically aware of this region as a cultural realm, until now known as some exotic paradise mortgaged to the travel agencies.

The scope of South Sea art is so vast (the label "Oceanic" compresses twenty cultures) that it would be incomplete to try a detailed analysis of it here, just as it would be insufficient to treat the history of Western European art in a phrase. South Sea art ranges from the ornate, rococo decorative styles of the New Zealand Maoris to the functional simplicity of the islands of Micronesia; from the expressionistic, semirealistic art of Easter Island to the imaginative symbolism of New Ireland carvings; from the metaphysical drawings of the Australian Bushmen to the abstract art of the New Guinea Papuans.

Yet if it is permissible to isolate the distinguishing character of an art tradition – if it is permissable, for example, to describe Western European art as an art of the voluptuous; if it can be said that the distinguishing character of Negro African art is that it is an art of terror, terror before nature as the idea of nature made itself manifest to them in terms of the jungle; if Mexican art can be said to contain a terror of power[3] –then it can be said that despite its wide range, the distinguishing character of Oceanic art, the quality that gives us a clue to its difference from all other art traditions, is its sense of magic. It is magic based on terror; but unlike the African terror before nature, this is a terror before nature's meaning, the terror involved in a search for answers to nature's mysterious forces.

All life is full of terror. The reason primitive art is so close to the modern mind is that we, living in times of the greatest terror the world has known, are in a position to appreciate the acute sensibility primitive man had for it. Yet though all men live in terror, it is the objects of terror that contain within themselves those elements of cultural interpretation that permit the differentiation of its various subjective expressions. Modern man is his own terror. To the Africa and to the Mexican, it was the jungle. To the South Sea Islander, it could not have been a like terror before an immobile nature, but a terror before forces, the mysterious forces of nature, the unpredictable sea and the whirlwind. In Oceania, terror is indefinable flux rather than tangible image. The sea and the wind, unlike the static forest and the jungle, approach metaphysical acts. Whether benign or catastrophic, they arise out of the mystery of space. The terror they engender is not, then, a terror before an inscrutable nature but one that arises before abstract forces. The Oceanic artist, in his attempt at an explanation of his world, found himself involved in an epistemology of intangibles. By coping with them, he developed a pictorial art that contained an extravagant drama – one might say a theater – of magic.[4]

The exhibition in New York was so arranged that each grouping showed a fraternity with the several facets of our modern art movements. The functionalism of Micronesian objects mirrors our own modern functional architecture and objects. It is very close to present constructivist concepts. The distortions of the Papuan shields and figures touch our abstract painters. Some of the distortions recall our expressionists. But the overwhelming evidence emphasizes that the main point of contact is with our surrealists.

We now know that for the surrealists and for those movements now arising out of surrealism the utopian dream was not what so many supposed, the Renaissance, but the art of the South Seas. The link, of course, is only one of emotional attachment. We know that, historically, the surrealists arrived at their statement through Freud. He was the catalyst who freed their unconscious selves to give them the hope that they might arrive through the free association of ideas and symbols at a magical world. They derived from him. Yet the relationship between South Sea art and surrealism makes clear that the modern painter, no matter of what school, is emotionally tied to primitive art. The Oceanic artist and the surrealist form a fraternity under a common fatherhood of aesthetic purpose.

Just as the exhibition clarified this fraternity, it also sharply exposed the fundamental cleavage between them, which explains why the surrealists failed to achieve this common purpose. It was almost as if the object lesson of this important exhibition was to demonstrate the failure of the surrealists correctly to interpret the meaning of magic – that they comprehended only its superficial aspects. By insisting on a materialistic presentation of it rather than a plastic one, by attempting to present a transcendental world in terms of realism, in terms of Renaissance plasticity and Renaissance space, by, so to speak, mixing the prevailing dream of the modern artist with the outworn dream of academic Europe, they hoped to make *acceptable* (the surrealists prefer the term sur-real) what they consciously knew was unreal. This realistic insistence, this attempt to make the unreal more real by an overemphasis on illusion, ultimately fails to penetrate beyond illusion; for having reached the point where we see through the illusion, we must come to the conclusion that it must have been illusion for the artists themselves, that they practiced illusion because they did not themselves feel the magic. For realism, even of the imaginative, is in the last analysis a deception. Realistic fantasy inevitably must become phantasmagoria, so that instead of creating a magical world, the surrealists succeeded only in illustrating it.

Here is the dividing line between the surrealist and the Oceanic artist. We know the primitive artist attempted no deception. He believed his magic. We feel it, too, because we can see that it came from deep convictions, that it was an expression of the artist's being rather than his beliefs. Without any attempts at illusion, working directly, using the plastic means per se, the primitive artist gives us his vision, complete and with candor.

There is a new movement that has arisen here in America which shows through its works that it has, in effect, reinterpreted Oceanic art, that it has also set out on an art of magic, but that this time it is a visionary art, a subjective art without illusionary trappings. Its techniques are the techniques of modern abstract art but its roots lie in the same mythological subject matter that motivated the South Sea artist. Its artists are thereby closer to him than the traditional surrealists. However, an analysis of the work of this group is the subject of another article.

Notes

1. David and Ingres, the French neoclassicists, had their dream in the Florentine Renaissance; Delacroix, leader of the French romantics, in the Renaissance through the flamboyant Rubens from Flanders; Manet, the French realist, found the Renaissance through the majestic, the baroque dream of Velázquez and Goya; while the Spanish realists, seeking to glorify the reality of their times in terms of an earlier idealism, went to the Renaissance directly. The list can be amplified to cover every major figure and school of European art, yet it would be dangerous to value it more seriously than as an interesting phenomenon in the history of artist psychology. There should be no dialectical insistence on a "historic process" lest some *Kunstwissenschaftler* more interested in the "grand" conception than in truth choose to indulge in it to build a dialectic of purpose to the delight of our Hegel-intoxicated generation. The significance of this romantic urge among artists is that it makes clear the psychological need they had and have for emotional security in a utopian dream based on the past. It is a search for a sense of fraternity. No more.

2. Europe and America have seen many grand exhibitions of African and Mexican art, but it is doubtful if South Sea art on such a scale has ever been shown anywhere.

3. The Mexicans carved the hardest stone without the benefit of metal tools and this victory over nature, this transcendental pride, is visible in the heroic monumentality of their work.

4. In many of the islands, art objects were made in religious exercises by a special elite class in special ceremonies depicting a specific mystery, and the objects then made were shown and destroyed immediately after the ceremony. Here religion was art and art was a religion.

* * *

7. The First Man Was an Artist

Published in the first issue of *Tiger's Eye*,[1] a short-lived magazine edited by the painter John Stephan and the poet Ruth Walgreen Stephan, this article asserts Newman's quest for a return to an original state of wholeness, when man sought to be creative before all else. He castigates modern science for its obsession with method rather than inquiry. Instead of asking the question 'what?', Newman declares, scientists ask 'why?'. The artist, unlike the scientist, asks questions fundamental to human existence – the primary questions. Art, Newman maintains, is a primary language, an outcry rather than a means of dialogue, and that outcry was a poetic expression, an instinctive outburst whose music conveyed meaning. Published in October 1947, Newman's description of tracing a stick through the mud in 'The First Man Was an Artist' foreshadows the originary gesture of *Onement I*, painted three months later. *JL*

1. Barnett Newman, 'The First Man Was an Artist',
Tiger's Eye, no.1, October 1947, pp.57–60.

A scientist has just caught the tail of another metaphor. Out of the Chinese dragon's teeth, piled high in harvest on the shelves of Shanghai's drugstores and deep in the Java mud, a half million years old, he has constructed Meganthropus palaeojavanicus, "man the great," the giant, who, the paleontologists now tell us, was our human ancestor. And for many, he has become more real than Cyclops, than the Giant of the Beanstalk. Those unconvinced by the poetic dream, who reject the child's fable, are now sure of a truth found today, 500,000 years old. Shall we artists quarrel with those who need to wait for the weights of scientific proof to believe in poetry? Or shall we let them enjoy their high adventure laid out in the mud and in drugstore teeth? For truth is for them at last the Truth.

Quarrel we must, for there is the implication in this paleontological find of another attempt to claim possession of the poetic gesture: that the scientist rather than the artist discovered the Giant. It is not enough for the artist to announce with arrogance his invincible position: that the job of the artist is not to discover the truth, but to fashion it, that the artist's work was done long ago. This position, superior as it may be, separates the artist from everyone else, declares his role against that of all. The quarrel here must include a critique of paleontology, an examination of the new sciences.

In the last sixty years, we have seen mushroom a vast cloud of "sciences" in the fields of culture, history, philosophy, psychology, economics, politics, aesthetics, in an ambitious attempt to claim the nonmaterial world. Why the invasion? Is it out of fear that its materialistic interpretation of physical phenomena, its narrow realm of physics and chemistry, may give science a minor historical position if, in the larger attempt to resolve the metaphysical mysteries, the physical world may take only a small place? Has science, in its attempt to dominate all realms of thought, been driven willy-nilly to act politically so that, by denying any place to the metaphysical world, it could give its own base of operations a sense of security? Like any state or church, science found the drive to conquer necessary to protect the security of its own state of physics. To accomplish this expansion, the scientist abandoned the revolutionary scientific act for a theological way of life.

The domination of science over the mind of modern man has been accomplished by the simple tactic of ignoring the prime scientific quest: the concern with its original question, *what?* When it was found that the use of this question to explore all knowledge was utopian, the scientist switched from an insistence on it to a roving position of using any question. It was easy for him to do so because he could thrive on the grip mathematical discipline had, as a romantic symbol of purity and perfection, on the mind of man. So intense is the reverence for this symbol, scientific method, that it has become the new theology. And the mechanics of this theology, so brilliant is the rhythm of its logic-rite, its identification of truth with proof, that it has overwhelmed the original ecstasy of scientific quest, scientific inquiry.

For there is a difference between method and inquiry. Scientific inquiry, from its beginnings, has perpetually asked a single and specific question, *what?* What is the rainbow, what is an atom, what a star? In the pursuit of this question, the physical sciences have built a realm of thought that has validity because the question is basic for the attainment of descriptive knowledge and permits a proper integration between its quest, the question *what* constantly maintained, and its tool, mathematics or logic, for the discovery of its answer. Scientific method, however, is free of the question. It can function on any question, or, as in mathematics, without a question. But the choice of quest, the kind of question, is the basis of the scientific act. That is why it is so pathetic to watch the scientist, so proud of his critical acumen, delude himself by the splendor of the ritual of method, which, concerned only with its own relentless ceremonial dance, casts its spell not only over the lay observer but also over the participating scientist, with its incessant drumbeat of proof.

Original man, what does it matter who he was, giant or pygmy? What was he? That is the question for a science of paleontology that would have meaning for us today. For if we knew what original man was, we could declare what today's man is not. Paleontology, by building a sentimental science around the question *who* (who was your great-grandfather?), cannot be excused for substituting this question for the real one, because, according to the articles of faith that make up scientific method, there is not, nor can there ever be, sufficient proof for positive answer. After all, paleontology, like the other nonmaterial sciences, has entered a realm where the only questions worth discussing are the questions that cannot be proved. We cannot excuse the abdication of its primal scientific responsibility because paleontology substituted the sentimental question *who* for the scientific *what*. Who cares who he was? What was the first man, was he a hunter, a toolmaker, a farmer, a priest, or a politician? Undoubtedly the first man was an artist.

A science of paleontology that sets forth this proposition can be written if it builds on the postulate that the aesthetic act always precedes the social one. The totemic act of wonder in front of the tiger-ancestor came before the act of murder. It is important to keep in mind that the necessity for dream is stronger than any utilitarian need. In the language of science, the necessity for understanding the unknowable comes before any desire to discover the unknown.

Man's first expression, like his first dream, was an aesthetic one. Speech was a poetic outcry rather than a demand for communication. Original man, shouting his consonants, did so in yells of awe and anger at his tragic state, at his own self-awareness and at his own helplessness before the void. Philologists and semioticians are beginning to accept the concept that if language is to be defined as the ability to communicate by means of signs, be they sounds or gestures, then language is an animal power. Anyone who has watched the common pigeon circle his female knows that she knows what he wants.

The human in language is literature, not communication. Man's first cry was a song. Man's first address to a neighbor was a cry of power and solemn weakness, not a request for a drink of water. Even the animal makes a futile attempt at poetry. Ornithologists explain the cock's crow as an ecstatic outburst of his power. The loon gliding lonesome over the lake, with whom is he communicating? The dog, alone, howls at the moon. Are we to say that the first man called the sun and the stars *God* as an act of communication and only after he had finished his day's labor? The myth came before the hunt. The purpose of man's first speech was an address to the unknowable. His behavior had its origin in his artistic nature.

Just as man's first speech was poetic before it became utilitarian, so man first built an idol of mud before he fashioned an ax. Man's hand traced the stick through the mud to make a line before he learned to throw the stick as a javelin. Archaeologists tell us that the ax head suggested the ax-head idol. Both are found in the same strata, so they must have been contemporaneous. True, perhaps, that the ax-head idol of stone could not have been carved without ax instruments, but this is a division in metier, not in time, since the mud figure anticipated both the stone figure and the ax. (A figure can be made out of mud, but an ax cannot.) The God image, not pottery, was the first manual act. It is the materialistic corruption of present-day anthropology that has tried to make men believe that original man fashioned pottery before he made sculpture. Pottery is the product of civilization. The artistic act is man's personal birthright.

The earliest written history of human desires proves that the meaning of the world cannot be found in the social act. An examination of the first chapter of Genesis offers a better key to the human dream. It was inconceivable to the archaic writer that original man, that Adam, was put on earth to be a toiler, to be a social animal. The writer's creative impulses told him that man's origin was that of an artist, and he set him up in a Garden of Eden close to the Tree of Knowledge, of right and wrong, in the highest sense of divine revelation. The fall of man was understood by the writer and his audience not as a fall from Utopia to struggle, as the sociologicians would have it, nor, as the religionists would have us believe, as a fall from Grace to Sin, but rather that Adam, by eating from the Tree of Knowledge, sought the creative life to be, like God, "a creator of worlds," to use Rashi's phrase, and was reduced to the life of toil only as a result of a jealous punishment.

In our inability to live the life of a creator can be found the meaning of the fall of man. It was a fall from the good, rather than from the abundant, life. And it is precisely here that the artist today is striving for a closer approach to the truth concerning original man than can be claimed by the paleontologist, for it is the poet and the artist who are concerned with the function of original man and who are trying to arrive at his creative state. What is the raison d'être, what is the explanation of the seemingly insane drive of man to be painter and poet if it is not an act of defiance against man's fall and an assertion that he return to the Adam of the Garden of Eden? For the artists are the first men.

***

8. The Sublime Is Now

This was the last of four contributions Newman made to *Tiger's Eye*, and was published almost a year after he painted *Onement I.*[1] He effectively summarises his previous ideas on the bankruptcy of the European tradition of painting. Beginning with an assessment of Greek art, moving on to the Renaissance and ending with Impressionism, he asserts that artists lost their ability to express the sublime, which he characterises as a 'relation to the Absolute', because of their concentration on beauty. The 'Absolute' was, perhaps, another term for the numinous. Being a Jew, Newman would have had a natural disinclination to nominate God but instead found a euphemism for the concept. Newman provides evidence of his familiarity with key philosophical texts by Longinus, Kant, Hegel and Burke. Finally, he declares that American artists are setting out to create paintings free of the weight of the history of art and that have subjectivity as their origin. The preposterousness of this statement, the idea that Newman could declare independence from the European tradition, may possibly be explained by the urgency of his desire to establish in the public mind a new national school whose leadership in the field of art paralleled the political and military position in which America found itself after the War. JL

1. Barnett Newman, 'The Sublime Is Now', in 'The Ideas of Art: 6 Opinions on What Is Sublime in Art?', *Tiger's Eye*, no.6, December 1948, pp.51–3

The invention of beauty by the Greeks, that is, their postulate of beauty as an ideal, has been the bugbear of European art and European aesthetic philosophies. Man's natural desire in the arts to express his relation to the Absolute became identified and confused with the absolutisms of perfect creations – with the fetish of quality – so that the European artist has been continually involved in the moral struggle between notions of beauty and the desire for sublimity.

The confusion can be seen sharply in Longinus, who, despite his knowledge of non-Grecian art, could not extricate himself from his platonic attitudes concerning beauty, from the problem of value, so that to him the feeling of exaltation became synonymous with the perfect statement – an objective rhetoric. But the confusion continued on in Kant, with his theory of transcendent perception, that the phenomenon is *more* than phenomenon; and in Hegel, who built a theory of beauty, in which the sublime is at the bottom of a structure of *kinds of beauty*, thus creating a range of hierarchies in a set of relationships to reality that is completely formal. (Only Edmund Burke insisted on a separation. Even though it is an unsophisticated and primitive one, it is a clear one and it would be interesting to know how closely the surrealists were influenced by it. To me Burke reads like a surrealist manual.)

The confusion in philosophy is but the reflection of the struggle that makes up the history of the plastic arts. To us today there is no doubt that Greek art is an insistence that the sense of exaltation is to be found in perfect form, that exaltation is the same as ideal sensibility – in contrast, for example, with the Gothic or baroque, in which the sublime consists of a desire to destroy form, where form can be formless.

The climax in this struggle between beauty and the sublime can best be examined inside the Renaissance and the reaction later against the Renaissance that is known as modern art. In the Renaissance the revival of the ideals of Greek beauty set the artists the task of rephrasing an accepted Christ legend in terms of absolute beauty as against the original Gothic ecstasy over the legend's evocation of the Absolute. And the Renaissance artists dressed up the traditional ecstasy in an even older tradition – that of eloquent nudity or rich velvet. It was no idle quip that moved Michelangelo to call himself a sculptor rather than a painter, for he knew that only in his sculpture could the desire for the grand statement of Christian sublimity be reached. He could despise with good reason the beauty cults who felt the Christ drama on a stage of rich velvets and brocades and beautifully textured flesh tints. Michelangelo knew that the meaning of the Greek humanities for his time involved making Christ the man into Christ who is God; that his plastic problem was neither the medieval one, to make a cathedral, nor the Greek one, to make a man like a god, but to make a cathedral out of a man. In doing so he set a standard for sublimity that the painting of his time could not reach. Instead, painting continued on its merry quest for a voluptuous art until in modern times the impressionists, disgusted with its inadequacy, began the movement to destroy the established rhetoric of beauty by the impressionist insistence on a surface of ugly strokes.

The impulse of modern art was this desire to destroy beauty. However, in discarding Renaissance notions of beauty, and without an adequate substitute for a sublime message, the impressionists were compelled to preoccupy themselves, in their struggle, with the culture values of their plastic history, so that instead of evoking a new way of experiencing life they were able only to make a transfer of values. By glorifying their own way of living, they were caught in the problem of what is really beautiful and could only make a restatement of their position on the general question of beauty; just as later the cubists, by their dada gestures of substituting a sheet of newspaper and sandpaper for both the velvet surfaces of the Renaissance and the impressionists, made a similar transfer of values instead of creating a new vision, and succeeded only in elevating the sheet of paper. So strong is the grip of the *rhetoric* of exaltation as an attitude in the large context of the European culture pattern that the elements of sublimity in the revolution we know as modern art, exist in its effort and energy to escape the pattern rather than in the realization of a new experience. Picasso's effort may be sublime but there is no doubt that his work is a preoccupation with the question of what is the nature of beauty. Even Mondrian, in his attempt to destroy the Renaissance picture by his insistence on pure subject matter, succeeded only is raising the white plane and the right angle into a realm of sublimity, where the sublime paradoxically becomes an absolute of perfect sensations. The geometry (perfection) swallowed up his metaphysics (his exaltation).

The failure of European art to achieve the sublime is due to this blind desire to exist inside the reality of sensation (the objective world, whether distorted or pure) and to build an art within a framework of pure plasticity (the Greek ideal of beauty, whether that plasticity be a romantic active surface or a classic stable one). In other words, modern art, caught without a sublime content, was incapable of creating a new sublime image and, unable to move away from the Renaissance imagery of figures and objects except by distortion or by denying it completely for an empty world of geometric formalisms – a *pure* rhetoric of abstract mathematical relationships – became enmeshed in a struggle over the nature of beauty: whether beauty was in nature or could be found without nature.

I believe that here in America, some of us, free from the weight of European culture, are finding the answer, by completely denying that art has any concern with the problem of beauty and where to find it. The question that now arises is how, if we are living in a time without a legend or mythos that can be called sublime, if we refuse to admit any exaltation in pure relations, if we refuse to live in the abstract, how can we be creating a sublime art?

We are reasserting man's natural desire for the exalted, for a concern with our relationship to the absolute emotions. We do not need the obsolete props of an outmoded and antiquated legend. We are creating images whose reality is self-evident and which are devoid of the props and crutches that evoke associations with outmoded images, both sublime and beautiful. We are freeing ourselves of the impediments of memory, association, nostalgia, legend, myth, or what have you, that have been the devices of Western European painting. Instead of making *cathedrals* out of Christ, man, or "life," we are making [them] out of ourselves, out of our own feelings. The image we produce is the self-evident one of revelation, real and concrete, that can be understood by anyone who will look at it without the nostalgic glasses of history.

* * *

9. Ohio, 1949

In August 1949, during a trip to Akron, Ohio, to visit Annalee Newman's family, Newman visited a number of sites of ancient Indian earthworks, such as at Fort Ancient in Warren County, Ohio. These visits inspired him to write an article that he never completed, in which he comes closest to voicing a phenomenological viewpoint. Newman's description of the mounds as pared-down works of art and his bodily experience of them evoke the experience he wanted the viewer to have of his own paintings. His experience of the mounds may have led him to scale up his work so that the viewer would be 'looking out as if inside a picture rather than outside contemplating any specific nature'. *JL*

Standing before the Miamisburg mound, or walking inside the Fort Ancient and Newark earthworks, surrounded by these simple walls made of mud, one is confounded by a multiplicity of sensations: that here are the greatest works of art on the American continent, before which the Mexican and Northwest Coast totem poles are hysterical, overemphasized monsters; that here in the seductive Ohio Valley are perhaps the greatest art monuments in the world, for somehow the Egyptian pyramid by comparison is nothing but an ornament – what difference if the shape is on a table, a pedestal, or lies immense on a desert? Here is the self-evident nature of the artistic act, its utter simplicity. There are no subjects – nothing that can be shown in a museum or even photographed; [it is] a work of art that cannot even be seen, so it is something that must be experienced there on the spot: The feeling [is] that here is the space; that these simple low mud walls make the space; that the space outside, the dramatic landscape looking out over a bridge one hundred feet high, the falling land, the chasms, the rivers, the farmlands and far-off hills are just picture postcards, and somehow one is looking out as if inside a picture rather than outside contemplating any specific nature. Suddenly one realizes that the sensation is not one of space or [of] an object in space. It has nothing to do with space and its manipulations. The sensation is the sensation of time – and all other multiple feelings vanish like the outside landscape.

What is all the clamor over space? The Renaissance deep space as a heroic stage, the impressionist flat space, cubist space, shallow space,

positive and negative space, trompe l'oeil enigmatic space, the pure space
– the space of "infinity" – of Mondrian's universe. There is so much talk
about space that one might think it is the subject matter of art, as if the
essence of musical composition were the question of whether Mozart
wrote in 3/4 or 4/8 time.

The love of space is there, and painting functions in space like
everything else because it is a communal fact – it can be held in common.
Only time can be felt in private. Space is common property. Only time is
personal, a private experience. That's what makes it so personal, so
important. Each person must feel it for himself. Space is the given fact of
art but irrelevant to any feeling except insofar as it involves the outside
world. Is this why all the critics insist on [space], as if all modern art were
an exercise and ritual of it? They insist on having it because, being outside,
it includes them, it makes the artist "concrete" and real because he
represents or invokes sensations in the material objects that exist in
space and can be *understood*.

The concern with space bores me. I insist on my experiences of
sensations in time – not in the *sense* of time but the physical *sensation*
of time.

* * *

10. Interview with David Sylvester

In April 1965 David Sylvester recorded interviews with two artists: Jasper
Johns and Barnett Newman. Sylvester, already a well-known critic, had
been slow to respond to and appreciate Abstract Expressionism but when
he finally did so he became one of its most eloquent supporters.
Sylvester's interview was broadcast in an edited version on BBC radio and
published in the *Listener* at the time of Newman's posthumous exhibition
at the Tate Gallery in 1972.[1] The interview arguably captured some of
Newman's most important observations on his own painting, including
his account of the genesis of *Onement I*, its relationship to his concept of

self and his sense of place. The version printed here is the re-edited version published shortly after Sylvester's death in 2001.[2] It differs in minor ways from the previously published text. *JL*

1. Newman, in Conversation with David Sylvester', *Listener*, vol.88, no.2263, 10 August 1972, pp.169–70.
2. Published in David Sylvester, *Interviews with American Artists*, Chatto and Windus, London 2001, pp.37–42.

David Sylvester **When was it that you first did a painting with one or two simple lines, horizontal or vertical, across the surface?**

Barnett Newman I would say that it began in '46–'47. In those years, whenever I did a painting with one or two elements in it, it did always have a sense of an atmospheric background, I suppose – with the exception of a painting which I called *Euclidean Abyss*, where the background is black and has some white coming through, but there's no true atmosphere; and where I move to the edge, a yellow edge with a corner in it. For me it's a historic painting in terms of my own history, because there for the first time I moved to the edge, and the edge becomes lighter than the central section. Ostensibly it should have ended where the dark part ends, but I moved further to the actual edge of the canvas, and I felt that I'd moved to the edge but hadn't fallen off. But the painting where I had only the one symmetrical line in the centre of the canvas – with no atmosphere – I did in 1948 on my birthday. Later I gave it the title *Onement*.

What led you to such an extreme kind of form?

I don't paint in terms of preconceived systems, and what happened there was that I'd done this painting and stopped in order to find out what I had done, and I actually lived with that painting for almost a year trying to understand it. I realised that I'd made a statement which was affecting me and which was, I suppose, the beginning of my present life, because from then on I had to give up any relation to nature, as seen. That doesn't mean that I think my things are mathematical or removed from life. By 'nature' I mean something very specific. I think that some abstractions – for example, Kandinsky's – are really nature paintings. The triangles and the spheres or circles could be bottles. They could be trees, or buildings. I think that in *Euclidean Abyss* and *Onement I* removed myself from nature. But I did not remove myself from life. And I think I got myself involved in what I began to realise was the true thing in relation to life for me, which in a sense was my life; and it became more personal.

In what way did that simple vertical give you this feeling that it related to your life? In a symbolic way? In a moral way?

Not in a moralistic way but in a moral way, in that it raised questions for me of the nature of myself in relation to the painting itself as an object, to the whole enterprise of painting as an activity. The problem of painting as a thing or as a window or as a vision of the world or as a living thing, and the moral crisis, I think, moved around the… It's hard to re-create the emotional equivalents of fifteen years back.

One thing does seem clear, I think. Up to then abstract painting seemed to present two distinct alternatives – the one using geometric forms and the one using free forms, biomorphic forms. Then you came along choosing neither alternative. A line that might have been straight was curved.

I don't think of it as a line, I think of it as a colour area that activates and gives life to the entire area of the painting. It's not a stylistic device, it's something that for me is more real. It permitted me to see myself and have a sense of my own reality. And that sense brings me to a deeper relation to the problem of nature. What we are actually trying to do is to say something that really is a metaphysical act, a metaphysical preoccupation in words, and it's not only difficult to talk about painting, but it's even more difficult to formulate an emotional complex which is tied up with a metaphysical experience, but I don't like to get involved really too deeply in these things, because they're hard to talk about without producing the impression that I'm involved in mysticism, which I'm not.

Let's consider the paintings with the narrow lines. You don't think of this vertical as a line; you think of it as a narrow band of colour. This, I take it, means that among other things you don't think of it as a line traversing a field but as a field between two other fields.

Yes. A field that brings to life the other fields, just as the other fields bring life to this so-called line. I think of line as a thing that involves certain possibilities. It acts as a contour and moves in relation to a shape; it also acts as something that divides space. Also one has to remember that, in relation to the problem of line, an artist can only make, or a human can only make, two kinds of line: he can make a straight line or he can make a curved line. It's possible to combine those things, and you get a sort of a zigzag or you get a combination of lines that create a sense of a shape. But to me there is a difference between a shape and a form, between a shape and a confrontation of an area. To verbalise and articulate what I think the line did to me, what *Onement* made me realise, is that I was confronted for the first time, I suppose, really with the thing that I did, whereas up until that moment I was able to remove myself from the act of painting, or from the painting itself. The painting was something that I was making, whereas somehow for the first time with this painting, the painting itself had a life of its own in a way that I don't think the others did, as much. I think that the paintings I did before this have a sense of life, but the thing I feel in relation to these paintings is that they are more removed, or most removed, from the problem of association with biomorphic or abstract shapes or any other kind of thing. I feel that I brought in a new way of seeing which could not have happened if I hadn't brought in a new way of drawing. I would like to make clear that I did not begin my old work or my newer work on the basis of a theoretical position, in relation to a way of drawing, a way of painting, a way of doing anything. I was fundamentally against all dogmatic positions. Having in my youth been an anarchist, a philosophical anarchist, I was against all dogmatic positions and I suppose that one way of describing my own feelings in relation to *Onement* is that it fortified me in this attitude towards life. It was a non-dogmatic painting, if that explains it. I don't really say you have to paint a painting by putting all of it in the centre. I don't really say there has to be a certain way, a certain size, that it has to be clean at the edges. I really don't know in that sense how to make a painting. I was once asked in the written symposium run by Tiger's Eye why I paint and I said: 'I paint so I'll have something to look at.' And sometimes I said: 'I write so I'll have something to read.'

One thing that I am involved in about painting is that the painting should give man a sense of place: that he knows he's there, so he's aware of himself. In that sense he relates to me when I made the painting because in that sense I was there. And one of the nicest things that anybody ever said about my work is when you yourself said that standing in front of my paintings you had a sense of your own scale. This is what I think you meant, and this is what I have tried to do: that the onlooker in front of my painting knows that he's there. To me, the sense of place not only has a mystery but has that sense of metaphysical fact.

I certainly do get a sense, which is quite extraordinary, of just that. Perhaps it is metaphysical because I find it very difficult to explain. In some odd way, the relations on the canvas between, say, two vertical areas of black in relation to an area of white give me a curious sense of having some rightness of placing in relation to my own possible gestures.

I hope that my painting has the impact of giving someone, as it did me, the feeling of his own totality, of his own separateness, of his own individuality, and at the same time of his connection to others, who are also separate. And this problem of our being involved in the sense of self which also moves in relation to other selves...The disdain for the self is something I don't quite understand. I think you can only feel others if you have some sense of your own being.

I think that one does get the feeling in front of your paintings of valuing one's own being, a certain sense of exhilaration in one's own being. One also has a sense of the otherness of the painting which is a separate presence from oneself. Obviously, people find cause for resentment in the fact that there are entities in the world other than themselves, and they need to accept the otherness of others.

Yes.

The experience of your painting would certainly seem to me to be an analogy of this, though I find it very difficult to explain, and I suspect that you find it difficult to explain.

I was just going to say that if you find it difficult to explain, I find it even more difficult to explain. I remember an incident during my first show, in 1950, where a friend of mine, a painter, got terribly upset and had tears in his eyes and began to abuse me. And I said: 'What's the trouble?' He said: 'You called me names, you made me aware of myself.' I said: 'Well, take it easy. I mean, everything is going to be all right.'

Why do you give some of your paintings titles such as *Adam*?

In titles I try to evoke the emotional complex I was under: for example, with one of the paintings, which I call *Vir Heroicus Sublimis*, that man can be or is sublime in his relation to his sense of being aware. I give paintings titles actually because I think they have some meaning. I try in the title to create a metaphor that will in some way correspond to what I think is the feeling and the meaning.

Does your sense of the feeling in a particular work come to you while painting it or after you're finished?

The verbalised title comes after I've finished. The test of the title naturally has to do with what I felt I was expressing at the time.

And while working on a painting are you conscious of developing that expression of a particular feeling?

When one becomes totally absorbed in the painting, the painting has a relation to one which is extremely complicated and, I think, quite profound. It would be impossible if I were in the middle of a painting for anybody to say: 'Well, what do you think of it? What do you call it?' At the same time, as the painting progresses and as it's finished, I do have a relation to it which in some way gives me the clue to its title. In other words, I'm not involved in formal exercises, so it's not a question of only giving it a title that is a handle for others to use. I think that the painting itself confronts me as a very particular thing, and I try to give it a title which for me evokes the emotional content, and I hope is a clue to others. But I do think that the paintings should have their impact in terms of their emotion without the title. I'm not illustrating an emotion. The problem of a painting is physical and metaphysical, the same as I think life is physical and metaphysical. It's no different, really, from one's feeling in relation to meeting another person. One has a reaction to the person physically; also I do believe that there's a metaphysical thing in the fact that people meet and see each other, and if a meeting of people is meaningful it affects both their lives. And to be able to say what really affects both their lives, as we are trying to do here, is extremely difficult.

But you *are* saying that the kind of sense of life which you feel in a painting is of the same order?

Yes. Otherwise we would be creating either fetishes or images or objects.

Recorded April 1965 in New York City. The version edited for broadcasting by the BBC was first published in the *Listener*, 10 August 1972. The present version has been edited from the transcript.

* * *

11. Statement in *Barnett Newman: The Stations of the Cross, Lema Sabachthani*

This statement was written for the catalogue of Newman's first museum exhibition that took place at the Solomon R. Guggenheim Museum in New York from April to June 1966. Newman had painted the first two works in 1958, a year after he had had his first heart attack and around the same time as he had painted *Outcry*. They have often been regarded as a private cry of pain. However, the group was also painted, and exhibited, at the time of the Vietnam war and has been interpreted as a memorial and as an oblique questioning of the morality of sending young Americans to battle in a distant land. More recently, claims have been made that *The Stations of the Cross* memorialise the Holocaust. Newman's *Stations* are a personal and public lament. *JL*

Lema Sabachthani – why? Why did you forsake me? Why forsake me? To what purpose? Why?

This is the Passion. This outcry of Jesus. Not the terrible walk up the Via Dolorosa, but the question that has no answer.

This overwhelming question that does not complain, makes today's talk of alienation, as if alienation were a modern invention, an embarrassment. This question that has no answer has been with us so long – since Jesus – since Abraham – since Adam – the original question.

Lema? To what purpose – is the unanswerable question of human suffering.

Can the Passion be expressed by a series of anecdotes, by fourteen sentimental illustrations? Do not the Stations tell of one event?

The first pilgrims walked the Via Dolorosa to identify themselves with the original moment, not to reduce it to a pious legend; nor even to worship the story of one man and his agony, but to stand witness to the story of each man's agony: the agony that is single, constant, unrelenting, willed – world without end.

The ones who are born to die
Against thy will art thou formed
Against thy will art thou born

Against thy will dost thou live

Against thy will die.

Jesus surely heard these words from the *Pirke Abot*, "The Wisdom of
the Fathers."

No one gets anybody's permission to be born. No one asks to live. Who
can say he has *more* permission than anybody else?

* * *

12. The Fourteen Stations of the Cross, 1958–1966

During the course of the exhibition at the Guggenheim, Newman
published a statement in *ARTnews*[1] that amplified the statement
published in the exhibition catalogue. He insists that the group of works
is not a sequential narrative but 'a single event'. *JL*

1. Barnett Newman, 'The 14 Stations of the Cross,
1958–1966', *ARTnews*, vol.65, no.3, May 1966,
pp.26–8 and 57

No one asked me to do these Stations of the Cross. They were not
commissioned by any church. They are not in the conventional sense
"church" art. But they do concern themselves with the Passion as I feel
and understand it; and what is even more significant for me, they can exist
without a church.

I began these paintings eight years ago the way I begin all my paintings
– by painting. It was while painting them that it came to me (I was on the
fourth one) that I had something particular here. It was at that moment
that the intensity that I felt the paintings had made me think of them as the
Stations of the Cross.

It is as I work that the work itself begins to have an effect on me. Just as
I affect the canvas, so does the canvas affect me.

From the very beginning I felt that I would do a series. However, I had
no intention of doing a theme with variations. Nor did I have any desire to
develop a technical device over and over. From the very beginning I felt

I had an important subject, and it was while working that it made itself clear to me that these works involved my understanding of the Passion. Just as the Passion is not a series of anecdotes but embodies a single event, so these fourteen paintings, even though each one is whole and separate in its immediacy, all together form a complete statement of a single subject. That is why I could not do them all at once, automatically, one after another. It took eight years. I used to do my other work and come back to these. When there was a spontaneous, inevitable urge to do them is when I did them.

The cry of *Lema* – for what purpose? – this is the Passion and this is what I have tried to evoke in these paintings.

Why fourteen? Why not one painting? The Passion is not a protest but a declaration. I had to explore its emotional complexity. That is, each painting is total and complete by itself, yet only the fourteen together make clear the wholeness of the single event.

As for the plastic challenge, could I maintain this cry in all its intensity and in every manner of its starkness? I felt compelled – my answer had to be – to use only raw canvas and to discard all color palettes. These paintings would depend only on the color that I could create myself. There would be no beguiling aesthetics to scrutinize. Each painting had to be seen – the visual impact had to be total, immediate – at once.

Raw canvas is not a recent invention. Pollock used it. Miró used it. Manet used it. I found that I needed to use it here not as a color among colors, not as if it were paper against which I would make a graphic image, or as colored cloth – batik – but that I had to make the material itself into true color – as white light – yellow light – black light. That was my "problem."

The white flash is the same raw canvas as the rest of the canvas. The yellow light is the same raw canvas as the other canvases.

And there was, of course, the "problem" of scale. I wished no monuments, no cathedrals. I wanted human scale for the human cry. Human size for the human scale.

Neither did I have a preconceived idea that I would execute and then give a title to. I wanted to hold emotion, not waste it in picturesque ecstasies. The cry, the unanswerable cry, is world without end. But a painting has to hold it, world without end, in its limits.

Further Reading

Exhibition catalogues

– Barnett Newman: The Stations of the Cross. Lema Sabachthani, Solomon R. Guggenheim Museum, New York 1966
– Michael Auping (ed.), Abstract Expressionism: The Critical Development, Albright Knox Art Gallery, Buffalo, in association with Abrams, New York 1987
– Yve-Alain Bois, 'Perceiving Newman' in Barnett Newman, Paintings, Pace Gallery, New York 1988, pp.1–13
– Yve-Alain Bois, 'Barnett Newman's Sublime=Tragedy' in Richard Francis (ed.), Negotiating Rapture: The Power of Art to Transform Lives, Museum of Contemporary Art, Chicago 1996, pp.137–48
– David Craven, 'Mythmaking in the McCarthy Period' in Mythmaking: Abstract Expressionist Painting from the United States, Tate Gallery, Liverpool, 1992, pp.7–42
– Georges Didi-Huberman, 'The Supposition of the Aura: The Now, the Then, and Modernity' in Richard Francis (ed.), Negotiating Rapture: the Power of Art to Transform Lives, Museum of Contemporary Art, Chicago 1996, pp.48–63
– Thomas B. Hess, Barnett Newman, Museum of Modern Art, New York 1971
– Jeremy Strick, 'Enacting Origins' in The Sublime is Now: The Early Work of Barnett Newman, Pace Wildenstein, New York 1994, pp.7–31
– Ann Temkin (ed.), Barnett Newman, Philadelphia Museum of Art and Tate, Philadelphia and London 2002

Journals and magazines

– Lawrence Alloway, 'The American Sublime', Living Arts, no.2, June 1963, pp.11–12
– Lawrence Alloway, 'Color, Culture, The Stations: Notes on the Barnett Newman Memorial Exhibition', Artforum, vol.10, no.4, December 1971, pp.31–9
– Nicholas Calas, 'Subject Matter in the Work of Barnett Newman', Arts Magazine, vol.42, no.2, November 1967, pp.38–40
– Ann Gibson, 'Barnett Newman and Alberto Giacometti', Issue: A Journal for the Arts, no.3, spring/summer 1985, pp.2–10
– E.C. Goossen, 'The Philosophic Line of B. Newman', ARTnews, vol.57, no.4, summer 1958, pp.30–1 and 62–3
– E.C. Goossen, 'The Big Canvas', Art International, vol.2, no.6, November 1958, pp.45–7
– Donald Judd, 'Barnett Newman', Studio International, vol.179, no.919, February 1970, pp.66–9
– Allan Kaprow, 'Impurity', ARTnews, vol.61, no.9, January 1963, pp.30–3 and 52–5
– Donald P. Kuspit, 'A Phenomenological Approach to Artistic Intention', Artforum, vol.12, no.5, January 1974, pp.46–53
– Barbara Reise, 'The Stance of Barnett Newman', Studio International, vol.179, no.919, February 1970, pp.49–63
– Robert Rosenblum, 'The Abstract Sublime', Artnews, vol.59, no.10, February 1961, pp.38–41, 56 and 58

Books

– David Anfam, Abstract Expressionism, Thames and Hudson, London 1990
– Andrew Benjamin (ed.), The Lyotard Reader, Oxford University Press, Oxford 1989, pp.196–211 and 240–9
– Briony Fer, On Abstract Art, Yale University Press, New Haven and London, 1997
– Serge Guilbault, How New York Stole the Idea of Modern Art. Abstract Expressionism, Freedom, and the Cold War, translated by Arthur Goldhammer, University of Chicago Press, Chicago and London 1983
– Thomas B. Hess, Barnett Newman, Walker, New York, 1969
– Francis Frascina (ed.), Pollock and After: The Critical Debate. Second Edition, Routledge, London and New York 2000
– Michael Leja, Reframing Abstract Expressionism: Subjectivity and Painting in the 1940s, Yale University Press, New Haven and London 1993
– Jeremy Lewison, Interpreting Pollock, Tate Gallery Publishing, London 1999
– Jeremy Lewison, 'Jackson Pollock and the Americanisation of Europe' in Kirk Varnedoe and Pepe Karmell (eds.), Jackson Pollock: New Approaches, Museum of Modern Art, New York 1999, pp.201–33
– John P. O'Neill (ed.), Barnett Newman: Selected Writings and Interviews, University of California Press, Berkeley and Los Angeles, 1990
– Alex Potts, The Sculptural Imagination: Figurative, Modernist, Minimalist, Yale University Press, New Haven and London 2000
– Harold Rosenberg, Barnett Newman, Abrams, New York 1978
– Robert Rosenblum, Modern Painting and the Northern Romantic Tradition. Friedrich to Rothko, Thames and Hudson, London 1975
– Gabrielle Schorr, The Prints of Barnett Newman, Verlag Gerd Hatje, Ostfildern-Ruit 1996
– Armin Zweite, Barnett Newman: Paintings, Sculpture, Works on Paper, Hatje Cantz, Ostfildern-Ruit 1999